William J Fay

REVELATION OF GOD

INTERNATIONAL THEOLOGICAL COMMENTARY

Fredrick Carlson Holmgren and George A. F. Knight
General Editors

Volumes now available

Joshua: Inheriting the Land
  by E. John Hamlin

Ezra and Nehemiah: Israel Alive Again
  by Fredrick Carlson Holmgren

Song of Songs and Jonah: Revelation of God
  by George A. F. Knight
  and Friedemann W. Golka

Isaiah 40–55: Servant Theology
  by George A. F. Knight

Isaiah 56–66: The New Israel
  by George A. F. Knight

Daniel: Signs and Wonders
  by Robert A. Anderson

Joel and Malachi: A Promise of Hope, A Call to Obedience
  by Graham Ogden
  and Richard R. Deutsch

Amos and Lamentations: God's People in Crisis
  by Robert Martin-Achard
  and S. Paul Re'emi

Nahum, Obadiah, and Esther: Israel among the Nations
  by Richard J. Coggins
  and S. Paul Re'emi

Habakkuk and Zephaniah: Wrath and Mercy
  by Mária Eszenyei Széles

Haggai and Zechariah: Rebuilding with Hope
  by Carroll Stuhlmueller

Forthcoming in 1988–89

Genesis 1–11
  by Donald Gowan

Isaiah 1–23
  by S. H. Widyapranawa

Isaiah 24–39
  by S. H. Widyapranawa

Jeremiah 1–25
  by Walter Brueggemann

Hosea
  by H. D. Beeby

Micah
  by Juan I. Alfaro

REVELATION OF GOD

A Commentary on the Books of

The Song of Songs
GEORGE A. F. KNIGHT

and

Jonah
FRIEDEMANN W. GOLKA

WM. B. EERDMANS PUBL. CO., GRAND RAPIDS

THE HANDSEL PRESS LTD, EDINBURGH

Copyright © 1988 by Wm. B. Eerdmans Publishing Company
First published 1988 by William B. Eerdmans Publishing Company,
255 Jefferson Ave. S.E., Grand Rapids, Michigan 49503

and
The Handsel Press Limited
33 Montgomery Street, Edinburgh EH7 5JX

Library of Congress Cataloging in Publication Data

Revelation of God.
(International theological commentary)
"A commentary on the books of the Song of Songs [by] George A. F. Knight
and Jonah [by] Friedemann W. Golka."
Includes bibliographies.
Contents: Revelation of love / George A. F. Knight—
Divine Repentance / Friedemann W. Golka
1. Bible.   O.T.   Song of Solomon—Commentaries.
2. Bible.   O.T.   Jonah—Commentaries.
I. Knight, George Angus Fulton, 1909-   .   Revelation of love. 1988.
II. Golka, Friedemann W.   Divine repentance.   1988.
III. Series.
BS1485.3.R48   1988   223'.907   87-27166

Eerdmans ISBN 0-8028-0336-9
Handsel ISBN 0 905312 74 0

CONTENTS

Abbreviations   vi

Editors' Preface   vii

REVELATION OF LOVE
  A Commentary on The Song of Songs   1

DIVINE REPENTANCE
  A Commentary on the Book of Jonah   65

ABBREVIATIONS

AV   Authorized Version
BDB   Brown-Driver-Briggs, *Hebrew and English Lexicon of the Old Testament*
ET   *Expository Times*
KJV   King James Version
LXX   Septuagint
mg.   marginal note
NEB   New English Bible
RSV   Revised Standard Version
TEV   Today's English Version
TDNT   *Theological Dictionary of the New Testament*

EDITORS' PREFACE

The Old Testament alive in the Church: this is the goal of the *International Theological Commentary*. Arising out of changing, unsettled times, this Scripture speaks with an authentic voice to our own troubled world. It witnesses to God's ongoing purpose and to his caring presence in the universe without ignoring those experiences of life that cause one to question his existence and love. This commentary series is written by front-rank scholars who treasure the life of faith.

Addressed to ministers and Christian educators, the *International Theological Commentary* moves beyond the usual critical-historical approach to the Bible and offers a *theological* interpretation of the Hebrew text. Thus, engaging larger textual units of the biblical writings, the authors of these volumes assist the reader in the appreciation of the theology underlying the text as well as its place in the thought of the Hebrew Scriptures. But more, since the Bible is the book of the believing community, its text has acquired ever more meaning through an ongoing interpretation. This growth of interpretation may be found both within the Bible itself and in the continuing scholarship of the Church.

Contributors to the *International Theological Commentary* are Christians—persons who affirm the witness of the New Testament concerning Jesus Christ. For Christians, the Bible is *one* scripture containing the Old and New Testaments. For this reason, a commentary on the Old Testament may not ignore the second part of the canon, namely, the New Testament.

Since its beginning, the Church has recognized a special relationship between the two Testaments. But the precise character of this bond has been difficult to define. The diversity of views represented in these publications makes us aware that the Church is not of one mind in expressing the "how" of this relationship. The authors of this series share a developing consensus that any serious explanation of the Old Testament's relationship to the New will uphold the integrity of the Old Testament. Even though Christianity is rooted in the soil of the Hebrew Scriptures, the biblical interpreter must take care lest he "christianize" these Scriptures.

Authors writing in this commentary series will, no doubt, hold various views concerning *how* the Old Testament relates to the New. No attempt has been made to dictate one viewpoint in this matter. With the whole Church, we are convinced that the relationship between the two Testaments is real and substantial. But we recognize also the diversity of opinions among Christian scholars when they attempt to articulate fully the nature of this relationship.

In addition to the Christian Church, there exists another people for whom the Old Testament is important, namely, the Jewish community. Both Jews and Christians claim the Hebrew Bible as Scripture. Jews believe that the basic teachings of this Scripture point toward, and are developed by, the Talmud, which assumed its present form about 500 C.E. On the other hand, Christians hold that the Old Testament finds its fulfillment in the New Testament. The Hebrew Bible, therefore, belongs to both the Church and the Synagogue.

Recent studies have demonstrated how profoundly early Christianity reflects a Jewish character. This fact is not surprising because the Christian movement arose out of the context of first-century Judaism. Further, Jesus himself was Jewish, as were the first Christians. It is to be expected, therefore, that Jewish and Christian interpretations of the Hebrew Bible will reveal similarities *and* disparities. Such is the case. The authors of the *International Theological Commentary* will refer to the various Jewish traditions that they consider important for an appreciation of the Old Testament text. Such references will enrich our understanding of certain biblical passages and, as an extra gift, offer us insight into the relationship of Judaism to early Christianity.

An important second aspect of the present series is its *international* character. In the past, Western church leaders were considered to be *the* leaders of the Church—at least by those living in the West! The theology and biblical exegesis done by these scholars dominated the thinking of the Church. Most commentaries were produced in the Western world and reflected the lifestyle, needs, and thoughts of its civilization. But the Christian Church is a worldwide community. People who belong to the universal Church reflect differing thoughts, needs, and lifestyles.

Today the fastest growing churches in the world are to be found, not in the West, but in Africa, Indonesia, South America, Korea, Taiwan, and elsewhere. By the end of the century, Christians in these areas will outnumber those who live in the West. In our age, especially, a commentary on the Bible must transcend the parochialism of Western civilization and be sensitive to issues that are the special problems of persons who live outside the "Christian" West, issues such as race relations, personal survival and fulfillment, liberation, revolution, famine, tyranny, disease, war, the poor, religion and state. Inspired by God, the authors of the Old Testament knew what life is like on the edge of existence. They addressed themselves to everyday people who often faced more than everyday problems. Refusing to limit God to the "spiritual," they portrayed him as one who heard and knew the cries of people in pain (see Exod. 3:7-8). The contributors to the *International Theological Commentary* are persons who prize the writings of these biblical authors as a word of life to our world today. They read the Hebrew Scriptures in the contexts of ancient Israel and our modern day.

The scholars selected as contributors underscore the international aspect of the Commentary. Representing very different geographical, ideological, and ecclesiastical backgrounds, they come from over seventeen countries. Besides scholars from such traditional countries as England, Scotland, France, Italy, Switzerland, Canada, New Zealand, Australia, South Africa, and the United States, contributors from the following places are included: Israel, Indonesia, India, Thailand, Singapore, Taiwan, and countries of Eastern Europe. Such diversity makes for richness of thought. Christian scholars living in Buddhist, Muslim, or Socialist lands may be able to offer the World Church insights into the biblical message—insights to which the scholarship of the West could be blind.

The proclamation of the biblical message is the focal concern of the *International Theological Commentary*. Generally speaking, the authors of these commentaries value the historical-critical studies of past scholars, but they are convinced that these studies by themselves are not enough. The Bible is more than an object of critical study; it is the revelation of God. In the written Word, God has disclosed himself and his will to humankind. Our authors see themselves as servants of the Word which, when rightly received, brings *shalom* to both the individual and the community.

—George A. F. Knight
—Fredrick Carlson Holmgren

REVELATION OF LOVE

A Commentary on
The Song of Songs

GEORGE A. F. KNIGHT

CONTENTS

Introduction   3

CHAPTER 1   10

CHAPTER 2   16

CHAPTER 3   20

CHAPTER 4   23

CHAPTER 5   28

CHAPTER 6   31

CHAPTER 7   36

CHAPTER 8   38

THEOLOGICAL IMPLICATIONS   46

Bibliography   62

INTRODUCTION

This book has two titles, *The Song of Songs,* and *The Song of Solomon.* Both titles are used in its heading. The book is a collection of some twenty-five love lyrics, or fragments of poems. Consequently, till recent times, the Church knew it as *Canticles,* from the Latin word for "songs." Their authorship is unknown. They were strung together by an editor in the latest period of the construction of the OT canon, possibly ca. 250 B.C. But since these poems, or some of them, were "traditional" and had been passed down by word of mouth possibly for centuries, their roots go well back into history, perhaps even to the days of Solomon (i.e., to the 10th cent.). But the editor has strung these separate poems together in a purposeful and creative manner whose significance it will be our deep interest to discover.

Two criticisms have been levelled at Songs, both of them moreover unworthy.

1. They are said to be full of allusions to the ancient myths that circulated in Canaanite culture, and about which we know a good deal since the discovery in 1928 of a whole library of epic poems and other material at Ugarit in what is now the State of Lebanon. This material has roots going back to the time of Moses. It contains stories about the lives and activities of gods and goddesses, whose love life was linked with the forces of nature and with the procreation of both animals and mankind. Through the influence of these poems men and women had come to regard the sex act as a means of worshipping the gods of nature. In fact, they believed they could ensure the "re-birth" of both animate and inanimate nature by inducing the autumn rains to come by means of what we today would call imitative magic. Nature would come to life when the divinities awoke from the sleep of death; this awakening was brought about by the act of human procreation. But our poems, while sometimes using ancient terms found in Canaanite theology, exhibited a new content by the 3rd century. Just as English speakers today can blithely speak of Wodensday and Thorsday without for a moment believing in the existence of these gods, so with the editor of our poems. Nowhere

in Songs is nature worshipped as such; it is always rejoiced in as the handiwork of Yahweh.

2. The poems are accused of being full of erotic imagery. Such may well have been the case when the poems were still young, and when Israel was fighting off the influence of Canaanite culture in its midst. Some Commentaries interpret Songs as if by 300-250 the vocabulary of the speakers meant the same then as it did a millennium earlier. For example, the Victorian era was sensitive to the issue of erotic suggestions that may mean nothing to us today. Thus, around the 1860s it was considered erotic to speak of the leg of a table! Some commentaries point to the ancient employment of the word "hand" in the OT when what was really implied was the male phallus. But who would apply such an interpretation to the expression "the hand of the LORD brought Israel out of Egypt"? The parts of the human body all possess names. These names may of course be used in a brothel. There they certainly convey or reveal a lust by the seeker after erotic experiences. But these same terms may also be used in a doctor's consulting room. There they occur in a creative manner. They are required so as to lead the doctor to the cure of disease and to effect the total welfare of the patient.

If Songs was "published" as late as the period of the Hellenistic Empire (i.e., after 331), then one reason for its issue may have been a protest against the actual cult of sex that the Greek civilization had brought to Palestine. The editor may have chosen deliberately to use the language of the culture that had been imposed upon the Covenant People and to employ it to the glory of God. (This we discuss later.) By so doing he may have been showing his faith in the basic revelation of God's plan for the world when—as he read in his Scriptures—in the beginning, by the power of the Spirit even as it brooded over chaos, God had brought forth by the utterance of his Word that Light which symbolized his creative love (Gen. 1:1-3).

When Jesus withdrew with his disciples into the "district of Caesarea Philippi," he was in fact leaving the borders of the "Holy Land." Caesarea was the Latin name for the ancient city of Dan. The Greeks learned to pronounce Dan as Pan, or as Paneas, the place where the god Pan especially was worshipped. By Jesus' day every form of sexual perversion was pursued there, in particular in an open theatre for all to view. Yet it was there, at that spot, that Jesus chose to put the question to his disciples, who must have been bewildered by what they saw: "Who do men say that the Son of man is?" (Matt. 16:13; Mark 8:27). We recall that the title "Son of man" (Jesus own interpretation of himself, not one given to him by others) means in

Hebrew "true, real humanity," and thus "man made in the image of God," i.e., *before* the Fall as reported two chapters later than Gen. 1:26. Though the NT passage does not say so explicitly, we can understand why Jesus chose Paneas to ask the questions that he put. He did so because the "total" answer he looked for must come forth from the "total depravity" brought about by the perverted use of sex—just as, in the beginning, Light had come from the mouth of God in order to answer the total Darkness.

The whole of the life of the natural world depends upon the fact of the relationship between the male and the female elements in its composition. This is true not just of animals, fish, and insects, but also of flowers and trees. One who grows any plant of the gourd family knows he or she must thrust the male "phallus" of its lovely yellow flower into the "vagina" of the female flower (thereby copying the divine Gardener) in order to obtain any fruit from it. We read how Jesus, in a natural manner, took the fact of this divinely ordained process to speak of Solomon, whose love-making is shown in Songs to be of a debased nature, as "not arrayed like one of these."

So we shall see as we study Songs how the ancient eroticisms have been sublimated during the period of our editor, and how these ancient expressions are now rendered instead to the glory of God. A commentary on Songs that takes time to analyze all such terms in detail is merely sterile. Robert Gordis keeps a good balance on this issue when, in the introduction to his commentary, he says: "The *Song* cannot be understood in isolation (from) the culture-pattern of the ancient Near East" (*The Song of Songs*, ix). We hasten to add that Songs cannot be understood in isolation from the rest of the OT canon!

Unlike work on the prophets, Songs does not have much—if any—history of the text. However, we are concerned to discover the date of its composition apart from placing it in its cultural setting. A Christian reader of Songs must remember that these poems are an important part of "the Scriptures" that were the only Bible of the early Church, and are referred to as such in the NT some forty-five times. 2 Timothy 3:16-17 declares that "all scripture is inspired by God . . . that the man of God may be complete, equipped for every good work." This reference, of course, is to the OT alone.

Most of the poems contain a vocabulary that was developing in the north of the country rather than in Judah; the place names that occur are of towns and mountains from northern Israel. We are dealing with the common folk of the countryside rather than with the sophisticated "upper classes" of Jerusalem or even of Samaria.

Again, the reluctance to use the divine Name is characteristic of the late period when the poems were collated.

Previous centuries, not possessing the critical tools that are in our possession today, took for granted that the poems were either by Solomon or about Solomon, that lascivious monarch of old. First, we are told at 1 Kgs. 4:32 that Solomon "also uttered three thousand proverbs; and his songs were a thousand and five." Second, Solomon was depicted as the great lover, in the sexual sense, on a par with Hercules (or Heracles), the sexually potent god of the Greeks. The latter was reputed to have impregnated seventy women in "one night of love." Solomon, we read, had access to a vast harem; he is remembered as having seven hundred wives and three hundred concubines (1 Kgs. 11:3). So he ought to be a man who, par excellence, would know the meaning of "love."

Proverbs 7:15-18, which is a link between the Wisdom section of the book of Proverbs and Songs, uses language that is identical with phrases that appear in Songs but that are employed for a description of adulterous "love." But as we shall see in the poems, Solomon's idea of love is scornfully dismissed as debasing and untrue. For, "his wives turned away his heart" (1 Kgs. 11:3).

3. There is a third point about Solomon, however, that we must connect with Songs. We read at 1 Kgs. 4:30 that "Solomon's wisdom surpassed the wisdom of all the people of the east." The rabbis who finally edited the books of the OT, at the end of the OT era, and who produced the canonical order of the books of the OT that we now take for granted, placed Songs in the third part of the Canon, among the "Writings"—alongside, for example, the book of Ecclesiastes. That book too had been attributed to Solomon, because it is a book of "Wisdom." Songs is thus to be classified with the Wisdom literature of the OT.

Too often we read that this section of the OT contributes little or nothing to our understanding of its theology. The scholars who make this assertion regard the Torah and the Prophets as the chief sources available to us as we seek to construct a theology of the OT. But again, as we shall see, by 300 Songs had become one of the chief vehicles within the canon of revelation, and thus it is a very important element in the OT for our understanding of the nature and purpose of God.

Jeremiah 33:10-11 informs us that even in Jeremiah's day, around 600, "there shall be heard again the voice of mirth and the voice of gladness, the voice of the bridegroom and the voice of the bride . . ." From this statement it is inferred that it was customary for poems such as we have in Songs to be sung at weddings. This may indeed have been so. Moreover, deriving from this reference, some modern interpreters of Songs have taken for granted that this is the key to understanding the setting of our book.

Up to the 19th cent. A.D. or so, particularly in Syria, Palestine's neighbor nation, a wedding ceremony could last for a whole week. During these festivities the happy couple, the bride and bridegroom, would be hailed as king and queen for the occasion, he being so named after the Solomon referred to in Songs 1.

We must accept that all this may, in fact, be an accurate memory of how some of the poems were used. But what those who interpret Songs in this way, by reference to the verse in Jer. 33, ignore is the *content* of that song he mentions. It includes reference to "the voices of those who sing, as they bring thank offerings to the house of the LORD: 'Give thanks to the LORD of hosts, for the LORD is good, for his steadfast love endures for ever!'" In other words, the song that the country folk sang at that point in history no longer referred merely to human love, but had become an expression of thanks to God, made in public worship, and employing the great refrain that occurs in Ps. 136. That psalm is all about the *hesed* of God, not of mankind—i.e., God's loyal, unchanging, steadfast love, which Israel had known since the days of Moses and which, by inference, had been the revelation of his creative purpose ever since the beginning of creation.

It is only late in Israel's experience of God's *hesed*, of course, that Israel's love poetry could be read in this way. Songs has many words whose meanings we find difficult to grasp because they may have been borrowed from the languages of the surrounding peoples (particularly the Egyptians), all of whom wrote love poems. Israel was now living at peace with its neighbors under the *Pax Persica* and so could now carry on trade and commerce. Some of the strange words in Songs also reveal that the Hebrew language had been developing from the preexilic days of "Classical Hebrew" to become the neo-Hebrew of postbiblical times.

This leads us to realize what both the Synagogue and the Church have known intuitively, that Songs is a book about God and not primarily about mankind. The sacredness of its character was affirmed at the Jewish council at Jamnia ca. A.D. 90, when it was declared to be part of the canon of the Bible. Jewish tradition since then has seen Songs as an allegory of the love of God for his Bride Israel. The result is that the Mishnah (*Yadayim* iii.5) can say: "For all the Writings are holy, but the Song of Songs is the Holy of Holies."

About the year A.D. 100 the great Rabbi Akiba said of Songs: "It defiles the hands," i.e., it was so holy that it could be accounted as being "of" God for his people Israel. To that end, the rabbis came to interpret every verse in Songs as referring to moments in Israel's history.

Christian tradition has seen Songs as an allegory of the love of Christ for his Church. These various interpretations sound rather ludicrous to us today. As he proceeds with his commentary on the Song of Songs in the Anchor Bible series, however, Marvin H. Pope wisely quotes from these Jewish and Christian allegories for our edification.

In the Middle Ages some expositors saw Songs as a dialogue between the human soul and the body. Such an interpretation, of course, depended on the Greek dualistic view of the nature of mankind. Such a view could have circulated only before the Reformers rediscovered the Hebraic view of the unity of the human person. The difficulty with an allegory, however, is that "anything can mean anything."

Although we today cannot accept these allegorical interpretations, they continue to remind us that a present-day critical analysis of the poems is not enough, nor is an anthropological appraisal of the sexual behavior of the ancient world helpful to us as heritors of the Scriptures. As it is, we can see that Songs would not have been included in the canon of Scripture if it had been seen to be only a collection of erotic poems. Our editor was a member of the Covenant People of God. He was not a Canaanite, nor was he a Greek, nor a Roman. He lived in the theocratic state that the post-exilic people had become, a people that not only knew but gladly sought to live out the commandments: "You shall have no other gods before me," and "You shall not commit adultery."

Thus we can see that, as the text of the canon grew and developed, so did "biblical criticism" within it. Songs clearly rejects such a verse as that in Prov. 31:3: "Give not your strength to women"; further it reinterprets such commandments as Exod. 22:16 and Deut. 22:28-29 in the light of Israel's developing awareness of God's covenant relationship with her as his Bride, even while it could continue to show the wondrous mystery of love that is mentioned at Prov. 30:18-19: "Three things are too wonderful for me . . . the way of a man with a maiden."

It has been said by historians that only one Roman emperor (Marcus Aurelius) over the several centuries of that empire remained completely faithful to his wife and she to him. Oscar Cullmann tells us that in Jesus' day a Gentile could be described as "a man without a father"; for Roman society, the occupying force in Judea in Jesus' day, was full of "solo mums," unmarried mothers. Homosexuality had always been rife in Greek society, and although many strong-minded individual women in the Hellenistic world rose to positions of power and authority, women as a whole were regarded by men as inferior beings. This continued to be so in most lands, particularly in the long history of China. Not so in Jewish society in Jesus' day. While men and women by nature had different functions in life, as our book of Songs reveals, each could react to the other and to God in identical ways on the ground that, as Genesis puts it: "God said, 'Let *us* make man, male and female, as one *adam*, in our image'" (Gen. 1:26-27 author's translation). This was a reality revealed to Israel alone, alone among all the nations, peoples, religions, customs, and societies of both the ancient world and of the present day.

In the days when an editor set the poems of Songs in an ordered sequence Israel was fully aware of its unique relationship to the God of gods, as that relationship was mediated through the bonds of the Covenant he had bestowed upon it. Consequently, when the "stock" of the wild vine, the gentile world, was grafted into the "choice (or 'true') vine, wholly of pure seed" (Jer. 2:21; LXX Greek *he ampelos he alethinos*) through the new covenant in Christ—himself the true vine—the youthful Church learned from the Synagogue that the Song of Songs actually reveals to us in its supreme loveliness that the nature of the God of the Bible is holy and creative love.

The Hebrew language uses different forms of the verb to indicate male and female; it is thus usually possible to conclude when it is HE or when it is SHE who speaks. (We shall use these two words in capital letters in the Commentary at the appropriate places.) Without further explanation, therefore, both of the two explain themselves in their own words.

What is most important of all to note is this. Our "sacred editor" has not just published for his own delight a collection of the love poetry he has enjoyed hearing and editing, as we might produce an anthology of verse today. He has not just shaken his poems together like peas in a cup and then offered them to his public in no particular order. He has placed his poems, by divine inspiration, in such an order that he is able, step by step, to show the meaning of true love. He thus reveals not just the love of a young human couple for each other, but actually the love of the living God. He alone is the source of the love they exhibit and which they discover to be more powerful and enduring even than death itself.

CHAPTER 1

1 **The Heading.** The title "Song of Songs" is the Hebrew way of saying "The best (or "the greatest") song" or, as Daniel Lys entitles his commentary, *Le plus beau chant de la création,* "the most beautiful song in creation." This Hebrew construction is paralleled in the phrase "holy of holies," meaning "holiest of all." Then again "It is Solomon's." This does not necessarily mean, as it might appear in English, that it was *by* Solomon. As in the biblical book of Psalms, a psalm entitled *le-Dawid* can indeed mean "by David." But it can also mean "in the style of David," or "in the Davidic manner." So here too. For Solomon was traditionally known (1) as having composed 1005 songs (1 Kgs. 4:32) and (2) as having been the great lover, for 1 Kgs. 11:3 remembers him as having had seven hundred wives and three hundred concubines—obviously round numbers, yet overwhelming enough! But there could be a third reason for appending Solomon's name to this collection of love poems: 2 Sam. 12:25 tells us that through Nathan the prophet the LORD himself "sent a message" to David about the baby that Bathsheba had borne him. "So he called his name Jedidiah, because of the LORD"; this name means "Beloved of the LORD." Then again, though Solomon is mentioned again at Songs 3:9, 11, his name occurs there in the third person, showing that he is not the author of the book.

From another point of view, however, the use of the name Solomon places Songs firmly in that third part of the Canon of the OT, the Writings. Songs is not part of Torah, the Law of Moses, nor was it written by one of the prophets. The fact that it begins with a heading like that of the book of Proverbs, "The Proverbs of Solomon," means that the final editor regarded it as being in the same category as the book of Proverbs, i.e., firmly allocated within the Wisdom Literature.

Incidentally, we note that Songs is a highly theological little book. This fact is not always taken into account by those who suggest that a "theology of the OT" can be discovered without the aid of the Wisdom Literature in general.

10

2-4 The fact that the Hebrew language has both masculine and feminine forms in the singular of its verbs is a help in determining who is speaking at any one time. From the original, then, we can determine on most occasions whether it is a HE or a SHE who is speaking, or even whether YOU is singular or plural, masculine or feminine. The two genders alternate throughout the collection of poems, enabling us to determine—in a manner not possible in English—the construction of each of the poems. We discover how the poem in question is to be taken as a whole or whether we must cut it into the sense sections that reveal whether it contains the utterance of one or more individuals. Yet on occasion we discover a WE speaking, reminding us that, like in a Greek chorus, a group of females appear at times to interject their thoughts into the one man-one woman dialogue from which the poems are largely built up. Here, at v. 4, the WE seem to be the "daughters of Jerusalem" who are mentioned at v. 5. These may well represent Solomon's harem of wives and concubines, though not all scholars agree about this identification.

This very first line (v. 2b) expresses the rapturous experience of a SHE who discovers she is falling in love, an experience known equally to both men and women. In fact, she declares that this is what is actually happening to her. In this verse, "for" is the Hebrew *ki,* which may well be rendered "(I declare) that . . ." She goes on, "Your love is sweeter than wine." We gather that *tob,* usually meaning "good," can mean "sweet," as it does in Ugaritic; the vocabulary of the latter is close to very early elements in the biblical book of Songs.

"Your name," she declares, "is oil poured out," giving forth its fragrance as it pours. In the OT a person's name represented him or her in person. In fact, it was almost like the modern use of the word "soul." One's personality, it was believed, was made evident even as the name was uttered. In a sense, one's character materialized when it was "poured out" over the lips. In Israel's early period a child would receive a name that would ideally describe his nature. This was true most noticeably when a grown man or woman, in later life, seemed to change in nature or entered into a new relationship to his environment, as when, e.g., he became a king. The same is true to this day in many cultures, such as that of Melanesia (cf. Gen. 32:28; Matt. 1:21). In the modern world the lover addresses the loved one by name again and again as they embrace—"Oh Mary, Oh Mary" and she exclaims "Oh John, Oh John." What SHE means is that "You are no Harry or Tom, you are uniquely John, my John, and no one else's."

11

Our author, however, appears to be approaching the subject of love only through a back door, so to speak. What we are shown here is not that true love such as John and Mary experience. Rather, it is merely an infatuation or perhaps even an erotic fantasy. We note that SHE supposes that lots of other girls are in love with HIM too! In her fantasy she sees herself being introduced to the royal harem, where she is welcomed by those already in it. The WE in v. 4c is no "royal we." The kings of Israel did not speak in such terms; the "you" in the Hebrew is in the feminine singular; and "your" love as understood by the Versions could be that of either male or female. Wine can, of course, "make the heart glad," but even imperfect love is "more than wine." Rather than "we will extol your love," some commentators believe we should read: "we will inhale your love" like the bouquet from the glass of wine.

5-6 It would seem that "Solomon" was holding a kind of beauty parade, and that SHE is hurt. At this event SHE addresses the harem. Moreover, the harem women seem now to have second thoughts about her. They reveal their "upper-class snobbishness" at the idea of a peasant girl being admitted to their ranks. Perhaps they are even revealing a degree of race prejudice. On the other hand, this is unlikely since the ancient world as a whole seemed not to have entertained that present-day evil which bedevils the peace of the world.

"I may be black (or "dark-skinned")," she says, "but I am pretty." All that the "macho" men present at the beauty parade are interested in is the female form. The result is that they elicit from her a self-centered and self-satisfied exclamation of her own estimation of herself.

What we have here is all that the "world" supposes love to be. We are shown that the wrong use of sex can result in (1) self-satisfaction at her own female beauty and, with the man, admiration for his male attributes. These views "miss the mark" (Hebrew *hata*, Greek *hamartanein*, both translated in the KJV or AV by the verb "to sin"). The woman is not meant to be used merely to gratify the male. Both of them miss out on God's great gift of *shalom*, attainable only through true love. (2) Young people today are encouraged by educationists in some places and by psychologists to "seek fulfilment of their personalities" by having intercourse with those with whom they experience "calf love." They must pander to their sexual needs or become introverted and morose. Yet such activities bring not *shalom* but *tohu*, that which is the opposite of *shalom*. *Tohu* is the emptiness of "nonbeing," that chaos mentioned in Gen. 1:2. What are popularly called "one-night stands" are not times of total self-giving of two persons, the one to the other, represented by the words of the marriage service in the Anglican prayer book, "With my body I thee worship."

SHE asks her hearers, then, to recognize that a girl may naturally be sunburnt through working in a vineyard in the country and yet still remain beautiful. Perhaps her brothers had given her the job of "keeper of the (family) vineyards." Again, perhaps they were jealous of her attractiveness, and treated her as a kind of Cinderella. The word "Kedar" is a general name for Arabian nomads, whose tents are brown in color; evidently, too, so were Solomon's curtains—while also being very sumptuous!

Those scholars who regard the background of the poems to be that of the sexual symbolism of the Canaanites and of the Egyptians are of course correct. Songs is filled with sexual innuendos. We can understand this since the explicit language throughout is found in such poems as those occurring in connection with the Ugaritic pantheon. That literature goes back to a thousand years before Songs was finally edited. Our poems had necessarily to use language common to the whole Near East. Yet here they are being employed within the OT canon. Consequently, they have become embodied in the literature of Israel's covenant faith. Thus, the line "but, my own vineyard I have not kept!" (v. 6d) may indeed have meant in earlier days simply "I admit, I am no virgin." Here, however, it must be taken at its face value, at what it meant to the New Israel after the Return from exile in Babylonia. (For such a judgment, see my volume, *The New Israel,* in the *International Theological Commentary.*) Her brothers, we have said, may have treated her poorly. They may have compelled her to work long hours in their own portions of the family vineyard, with the result that she was forced to neglect that section of it which was her own heritage.

7-8 These verses act as a kind of bridge between the "harem" story of vv. 1-6 and what follows. SHE had been infatuated with King Solomon and with the thought of living in the harem. This is no more surprising to read about than the fact that today thousands of teenage girls may entertain an infatuation for a good-looking actor whom they see only on the screen, or a sensuous pop singer whom they listen to with avidity. Fortunately, such girls grow out of their fantasies.

The poem thus sees her growing out of her ridiculous situation. For this king she admires is a son of David the shepherd king; thus,

conceivably under the influence of her religious upbringing, she re-
vises her dreams and envisions her beloved rather as a shepherd. She
might now seek him out at the noon break when they stopped for
lunch in the heat of the day. She has no wish, however, to be regarded as a prostitute who "wanders" near the shepherds. Such a
female has necessarily forfeited every expectancy of true love.

It is a mistake to translate the Hebrew word *nephesh* by "soul."
The modern Western reader is imbued with the view, derived from
Greek philosophy and not from the Scriptures, that "mankind has a
soul." Hebrew *nephesh* describes the human as being a whole, total
person, "body, soul, and spirit," as it were. Thus, love is not something etherial, as it appeared to the artists of the romantic revival two
centuries ago. They pictured love as a sentiment known to shepherds
and shepherdesses in the Elysian fields. We must remember this as,
bit by bit in these poems, we are shown what human love can really
mean, and what it is meant to be. For the human *nephesh* involves
the body as well as the "soul," and although God is nowhere mentioned explicitly in the poems, *nephesh* implies the presence of the
Good Shepherd himself in the human relationship of love. So in v. 8
SHE is told (by the chorus?) to pursue the search for her Shepherd
assiduously.

9-17 This is a separate poem completely. The editor of the whole
collection has placed it here with a purpose. HE (Mister Right, as
teenage girls say today?) and SHE have now met. No longer is Solomon the object of this young woman's dreams. This girl has met her
social equal—a fellow countryman, an ordinary human being, a son
of the soil—and they have fallen in love in the manner that is in accordance with the mind and plan of God for his creatures, male and
female.

In vv. 9-11 HE speaks. We need hardly comment on his choice of
language. He is ecstatic at finding that true love is not of the "soul"
but of the whole *nephesh*. And here our Hebraic heritage has something unique to offer to Western society, which for many years has
been dominated by its Greek heritage. The latter separates the ideal
from the actual, heaven from earth, time from eternity, body from
soul, male from female, love from sex; this separation has brought
about in the West the promiscuous and permissive society that the
rest of the world despises.

Verses 12-14 are in the form of a dialogue. In v. 12 SHE speaks
of her beloved as a king. In this manner the editor has been able to
link this poem with the introductory poems in vv. 1-8. In v. 13 HE

replies. Each outdoes the other, using poetic language that can translate into the languages of cultures of all peoples. All young people everywhere know what it means to fall in love. SHE rests in his arms. In v. 14 En-gedi (literally, "kid well" or "spring of the kid") was a well-known spot on the west bank of the Dead Sea. Its isolated spring of fresh water produces a welcome oasis in the wilderness behind and above it, one that was known throughout the whole of biblical history.

In v. 15 HE says to HER what all real lovers find to be true, that his beloved can be described only in the language of poetry. In v. 16 SHE replies in similar terms, only now with a different word for "beloved," one that is perhaps well rendered by "darling." It may be that what follows they say together, since the verbs do not show their gender. The arbor HE has built for HER to dally in is as if it were a palace of cedar and pine.

Incidentally, we note with interest that neither HE nor SHE ever says "I love you," a phrase we would expect. Always, and in both cases, it is "you" who takes precedence over "I." Their love for each other is not based on self, but is wholly dependent upon the other. Thus they can quite naturally speak of "our . . ."

CHAPTER 2

1-3 HIS sincere devotion to HER makes the woman ask herself what there is in her to elicit love in this way. In other words, his love for her awakens in her a new self-respect. The SHE of 1:5-6 was doubtful about any attractiveness she may have had. The SHE here, on the other hand, as the object of HIS love, now glows with a radiance that all can see. Yes, we can always pick out a lover in a crowd as we notice how her face is aglow.

Sexual attraction is a natural element in the human constitution. It was the body with all its instincts that God created first. Only thereafter did he employ the physical frame that he had formed to incarnate the power of the Spirit (Gen. 2:7).

Sharon in the early days of the Israelite kingdoms, lying near the shores of the Mediterranean, had been unproductive land of old. It had had to be circumvented by marching armies. In those days it was marshy and boggy. By now, however, it had been drained, and so came to be known as that area which produced the best wheat. In other words, Sharon was now the most productive area in the Holy Land, and there too the fairest wildflowers flourished. The Hebrew word *shoshannah* (from which we get the name Susanna) means some kind of beautiful wild flower, probably a lily, but the word *habatstselet* (RSV "rose") describes a flower we are unable to identify. Some say it was a crocus, some an asphodel. But the name "rose of Sharon" is a beautiful one and has become embedded in English literature. From our point of view, a rose is a much more beautiful flower than a crocus. So let it stand!

We note again and again how Songs makes full use of symbolism: "I am (like) a rose of Sharon." "(He is like) an apple tree." Symbolism can express nuances beyond the power of so-called exact definition, as Robert Gordis says in his commentary (p. 37), and is much more profound than allegory. This is important for any discussion of the theological significance of the poems, a theme we shall handle later.

I am so far different from my girlfriends as a lily is from prickly brambles, SHE continues. As for her beloved lover, HE stands out from his companions as an apple tree does in all its fruitfulness and rosy-cheeked attractiveness when one comes across it unexpectedly as it grows among mere scrub or brushwood. Then, in his care for her, she declares, he made sure he sheltered her from the hot Near Eastern sun (a phrase used of God's care for his people in Ps. 17:8; 36:7; 57:1, etc), and his kisses were sweet to her palate.

From Songs 2:4 there follows a passage often quoted in English literature. Their simple bower beside a vineyard (literally, "house of wine") was for them a banqueting house, for one reason only: "his banner over me was love." We need not dissect that line of verse, but just rejoice to learn that the experience of true love is "very heaven."

Here again our Hebrew poet parts company with his Greek contemporary. He does not separate "heaven" and "earth." God, he believes with the authors of Genesis, has made them both one. Yet we experience them as being both separate, because they are separated indeed. They are separated by sin. Here, however, both HE and SHE can "taste and see that the LORD is good!" (Ps. 34:8). They have discovered that it is not goodness that is the opposite of evil, but rather love that is its opposite, and love is of God himself. Moreover, "it is characteristic of the delicacy of the songs that the woman in each case expresses her desire for love by indirection . . . . The use of symbolism, which conceals as it reveals, heightens by its subtlety the charm of the sentiments expressed" (Gordis, 38). There is none of what Jesus refers to when he declares: "I say to you that every one who looks at a woman lustfully has already committed adultery with her in his heart" (Matt. 5:28).

Songs 2:6b can be expressed in simple English: "His right hand held me tight." There is no "O that . . ." of the RSV in the Hebrew. At v. 7 we are reminded once more that what we are reading is love poetry. The chorus, which we identified at 1:4 with Solomon's harem, again speaks for all of us as we behold the couple in their loving embrace. As we say today: "All the world loves a lover." So the "daughters of Jerusalem" here seem to speak for all mankind as well as for the ministering angels that are hovering over their bower (see the NEB translation).

Jewish tradition declares that just as a *huppah*, a canopy, is stretched over the marriage bed, so the *shekinah*, the immediate presence of the holy God, hovers over any young couple as they embrace in married love (cf. Isa. 4:5; Joel 2:16; Ps. 19:6, where a bridegroom "leaving his chamber" is "emerging from under his canopy"). "Leave them alone" in their privacy, commands the chorus. Consequently, we today add to their command: "Those whom God has joined together, let not man put asunder"—including either one of the couple themselves!

8-13 These lines are not in continuity with the above. They form a separate poem and deal with a different occasion. The poem is a true love song. It refers to the enchanting days of courting when each is learning daily more of the mysteries and excitements of love.

SHE is at home with her mother, perhaps sewing her trousseau! All at once she hears his voice, and up she leaps in joy. With poetic imagination she describes his coming in terms of a gazelle leaping upon the mountains. The mountaintops, in cultures everywhere, represent joy and lightheartedness. We ask a friend, "How are you today?" and he replies, "Oh, up in the clouds." Such is his mental state. But next day he may reply, "I am down in the depths." Biblical imagery is similar. When one is sick, one is "in Sheol," down in the depths below the level of true human living. But treading upon the mountaintops represents a joyous "heavenly" experience. Habakkuk shows his utter faith in God by declaring that even if all nature should fail and famine stalk the land, "yet I will rejoice in the LORD . . . he makes my feet like hinds' feet, he makes me tread upon my high places" (Hab. 3:17-19). See the powerful exegesis of this passage in Maria Eszenyei Széles' commentary, *Wrath and Mercy,* in the *International Theological Commentary.*

There HE is, "behind our wall, gazing in at the windows, looking through the lattice." Of course, in those days glass had not yet been invented; lattices were used like those in certain Near Eastern arabesque houses to this day. Through a lattice HE calls to HER to come out and fly away with him among the glories of the spring foliage. We need say no more. We cannot improve upon the loveliness of this passage.

14 This verse forms a separate snatch of song. It contains more in it than meets the eye. It has been written by a person who knows his Psalter.

HE addresses his beloved as a "dove," a wild pigeon that lives in the clefts of the rock, in the covert of the cliff. A dove is a gentle creature, and as such is comparatively defenseless and can well use the aid of humans to guard its shelter. This is just what Israel asks of God. Psalm 74:19 reads: "Do not deliver the *nephesh* (the soul, the life) of thy dove to the wild beasts." This line is then paralleled with: "Do not forget the life of thy poor for ever." "Life" and "wild beasts" use the same consonants. Hebrew poetry, just as later on Arabic poetry has done, compresses two or even three ideas together in this way by the use of puns.

Hebrew has two names for a (turtle) dove, just as has English. At Songs 2:14 the word HE uses of his beloved is *yonah*. At once we recall the story of the prophet Jonah and how, though very rebellious, God would not let him go till he learned to know and obey him even in a foreign land. This was Israel's task when, in exile in Babylonia, they suffered for their rebelliousness. (See my *Ruth and Jonah*.) That Israel was God's beloved is a reality that is basic to our understanding of the Song of Songs. We discuss this issue later.

15 Verse 15 is a one-verse chorus line. The onlookers, it seems, the daughters of Jerusalem or perhaps the heavenly choir, reveal their anxiety to protect the Bride. Their poem is a prayer. They ask God (?), who uses only human hands, to catch the foxes, and then in parallel "the little foxes." Surely these represent the nagging forces that militate against the young couple's love-making. If the foxes spoil the vineyards, then they could as easily seize "my dove . . . in the covert of the cliff."

16-17 The complete mutuality of their love is expressed in this fraction of a poem. This is an important point to note. HE is not the dominant partner; his approach to her is not of the "macho" variety that the Western world, basing its ethics and culture upon the myths of the Greeks, holds dear. Nor is SHE the mere subservient partner. Together they represent the divine ideal, as when the HE in the Garden exclaimed in ecstasy, when God "brought HER to the man": "This at last is bone of my bones and flesh of my flesh" (Gen. 2:23).

Moreover, since it is SHE who speaks here, she is expressing the same utter satisfaction that HE expressed in the Garden. The Garden is now nature in all its glorious beauty, "until the day sighs and the shadows flee away" (Songs 4:6, author's translation), and her beloved, exulting in his love, leaps with joy upon the heights of the hills (cf. 2:8).

CHAPTER 3

1-4 The path of true love never runs smoothly. Every young lover must find this out for him or herself. In love there is always pain, pain that is experienced also by the One who loves us.

These verses are poetry. They may not describe an actual event. They tell of an agonizing dream that SHE experienced, perhaps a recurring nightmare. But how vivid is the story. We see her distraught, searching for him from room to room, then into the barns and vineyards of the family property, finally through the streets and the squares of their small town. Agonizedly she turns to the night watchmen, the police patrol as we would call them: "Have you seen my true love?" Obviously true love must be tested to discover our fidelity to each other and to the God of love. It is possible that when trials come upon us we collapse inwards like deflated balloons. But God's creative love is offered to us, not to defeat us, but that we might be strengthened to meet the vicissitudes of life and love and then, in the end, to come out victorious.

There HE is then, emerging from the dark of the night. Oh, the unutterable peace and joy she feels. So he has not abandoned her. He is still her one and only beloved. SHE clings to him and takes him back home with her to the bosom of her family. Many Christian commentators in later centuries read into the simple Hebrew form *kim'at* ("scarcely") the idea of "Seek and ye shall find," and suggested that God grants his love only when he sees that we truly desire it. But this interpretation is not in tune with the total biblical revelation, for in it we learn that "He loved us before we loved him." In fact, this little poem is not to be read allegorically. It is an expression in agonizingly revealing terms of the simple fact of the pain that is always present in true love.

5 Once again, in language identical with 2:7, the blessing of the God of love is spoken by the chorus of female voices. How inspired the editor of this collection of love poems has been in his placing of even little portions of poems in the order he has chosen for his purpose. The young couple's love-making clearly has her mother's full approval and blessing.

6-11 The editor has assumed it wise to contrast at this point the pomp and worldliness of a royal wedding with the simplicity and holiness of the union of two lovers from a village situation. These qualities are God's gifts to any ordinary young couple who rejoice in all the kindly affection shown by the neighbors. HE, in his own small way, is hailed as Solomon for the day. By reverting in ch. 4 to a description of true love, the editor thus deliberately shows that "Solomon in all his glory was not arrayed like one of these." Our couple were truly as simply and beautifully clad as the lillies of the field that anyone could pluck (2:1; Matt. 6:28-29).

The royal caravan is so extended that one can see from afar the dust raised by the hooves and wheels of Solomon's many attending vehicles with their caparisoned horses. They are "coming up from the wilderness," presumably to Jerusalem; the verb *'alah* ("go up") has been used to this day of the thousand meter ascent to the Holy City by pilgrims making the journey for the festivals, and of returning Israelites from the Diaspora to the ancient Land of Promise.

At its center is the royal litter, with the king lolling in comfort on his cushions, all powdered and perfumed with frankincense and myrrh. The choice of word for litter, Hebrew *mittah,* may in fact be a rather vulgar usage, since it could apply to a double bed ready to be used by two persons when the king takes his next consort under its canopy.

Despite his name *Shelomoh,* which is built from the word for peace, *shalom,* HE comes attended by "sixty mighty men . . . all girt with swords and expert in war, each with his sword at his thigh, against alarms by night." We note that SHE rejects such macho lovemaking, confounded as it was with the brutality of war. Solomon had exploited the glorious forest of Lebanon to have his palanquin fashioned of its beautiful cedar wood. The palanquin itself probably would have been decorated by the fair hands of his harem ladies, and so now would be Solomon's pride and joy. The silver of its posts could only have derived from trade with a far country, and so too with its golden "back." We know that Solomon taxed his people heavily, so it was they who really paid for his glorious "hobby horse." The word "back" may represent a high pillow or bolster ornamented with gold lace. Its "seat" again was probably a cushion. The RSV's doubt about the following line lets us translate with the NEB "its lining was of leather." It was G. R. Driver who first suggested that the word for "love" here might be read as "leather" ("Supposed Arabisms in the Old Testament," *JBL* 55 [1936]: 111); since that article commentators have sought to describe the interior of such a palanquin by showing that it would be painted with baskets of flowers, around them being mottos about love.

Is this picture of human glory meant to contrast with that of Yahweh, whose glory is that of creative love? The word "column" (Hebrew *timerah*), in "a column of smoke" (v. 6a), as Marvin H. Pope points out (*Song of Songs*, 426), is apparently a synonym for ʿ*ammud,* the pillar or column that is applied to the pillars of fire and cloud symbolizing the presence of the Lord preceding the Israelites in the desert (Exod. 13:21-22; 14:19, 24; Neh. 9:12, 19; cf. Isa. 19:1; Ps. 68:4). Then the word *lebonah,* "frankincense," used to glorify Solomon, is perhaps meant to contrast with the name *Lebanon,* the "white" mountain that glorifies the Lord of creation. The NEB again may be correct in translating, where the RSV has "against alarms by night," "to ward off the demon of the night." True love, our editor may be explaining, does not need to fear any night demon, for the Shekinah hovers over the marriage bed of those who love with the love of God, revealed as it is in his relationship with his covenant people (cf. Ps. 136).

Songs 3:11 gives us the words of the poet as he calls upon the "daughters of Zion," the chorus, perhaps along with the young girls from the city as well, to come forth—from the harem? They are to behold Solomon as he approaches for his latest wedding. When Solomon came to the throne at the death of his father David, it was only with the help of his mother Bathsheba that he did so (1 Kgs. 1). According to the biblical record, his first wife was a daughter of the current pharaoh of Egypt. This, of course, was an "arranged" marriage, a "mariage de convenance" and not a love marriage. We can well imagine how the court at Jerusalem would provide a magnificent reception for the Egyptian bride, in their loyal attempt to make her wedding as splendid as any that a pharaoh could offer his daughter. Bathsheba, the doting queen mother, would probably have presented her son with the crown that is mentioned here. Was it then used at the celebration of all Solomon's subsequent marriages? This may have been why the custom seems to have been perpetuated down the centuries, the bride and bridegroom being crowned with a garland of flowers even at an ordinary village wedding.

CHAPTER 4

1-7 HIS poem. A love poem such as this needs little analysis. It contains poetry that could have been composed and recited in many countries of the world. What our editor is emphasizing is that love is not the possession exclusive to the chosen people, but can be experienced by all mankind. However, here it is tied down to Palestine specifically by its references, few as they are. Probably, the poems that the editor has strung together here were common property and had been so even for several centuries; quite possibly, snatches of these lines were remembered here and there so that they passed unnoticed from one singer to another. Again, as a number of scholars suggest, they were remembered in particular because they were sung on the occasion of a festive wedding party or at a feast.

"Gilead" is an area southeast of the Lake of Galilee. It receives rather more rain than does the region further south. So it is more productive, is greener, and is famed for its sheep and cattle.

2 "Come up from the washing" is better read "from the dipping." The ewes were evidently healthy: because if they bore twins, then they had sufficient milk to feed both lambs.

4 "Your neck is like the tower of David" does not sound very complimentary to us in our culture; nor does "built for an arsenal" add much help. The image is of a commanding tower in the Holy City, adorned with trophies of war (cf. Ezek. 27:11). Perhaps this tower is the one mentioned at Neh. 3:25-26: "the tower projecting from the upper house of the king at the court of the guard." Yet this tower must have pleased the sensibilities of the people of that day and have struck them as architecturally beautiful. There are tribes in old Africa and in South America that see in an artificially stretched female neck something attractive to the male.

Thus, instead of the word "arsenal" (see RSV margin) the suggestion of A. M. Honeyman ("Two Contributions to Canaanite Topography," *JTS* 50 [1949]: 50-51) may be the answer we seek. He suggests that the Hebrew word comes to mean "to arrange in courses," so that the tower was "built of coursed masonry," in which case the lady may have worn several strings to her necklace. At Songs 7:4 once again her neck "is like an ivory tower." We are to remember that we are seeing this beloved one through the eyes of her lover. Every lover sees his beloved as "a perfect angel." Our bridegroom sees his bride as "all fair, my love; there is no flaw in you" (4:7).

8 This verse seems to be part of another rhapsodic poem, not dependent upon the one before. It is full of place names. Lebanon is the great snowcapped mountain to the north of Palestine, from which the modern state derives its name. Hermon is the mountain to its east, on the other side of a deep valley that cuts between them. Amana is not mentioned elsewhere in the Bible, but it may be assumed to be another spelling of Abana, the "river of Damascus" mentioned at 2 Kgs. 5:12. The reference is probably to the heights from which it flows. Senir seems to be one of the peaks of Mt. Hermon. All these mountain areas were inhabited in OT times by wild beasts such as the lions and leopards mentioned here.

9-15 This is another independent poem, placed here by the editor to continue the ecstatic descriptions made by HIM of the loveliness and beauty of the girl he adores.

Once again, the poem speaks for itself. Naturally, however, SHE is not HIS sister in a literal sense. "Sister" and "bride" are synonyms in these poems; he is clearly searching for words of endearment. The NEB has selected the Greek (LXX) rendering, *ekardiosas*, "you have put heart into me," over the reading of the Hebrew verb *libbabtani*, which occurs in the piel. If this is the better sense of the original verb, as it seems to be in this context, then it means that her love for him has contributed to create love in his heart. He recognizes the reality that love is indeed creative and that it produces and fosters love in the one who is loved. Moreover, since this action is mutual, the result of their mutual love is a whole new quality of life. It is one that they hold in common, yet which is unknown to and unattainable by those who have never loved. Songs is thus showing that Solomon could never have known this kind of love. Consequently, at this point, the contrast between him and his relationship to his harem and that of our young couple-in-love is manifest. Solomon's so-called "love" was only a mixture of infatuation and lust.

The reference to "honey and milk" at v. 11 may be an echo of that deeper meaning of Songs which both Jews and Christians have found in it. In Dan. 11:16, 41, 45 Israel's land, known as the Promised Land—promised by Yahweh ever since Abraham's day (Gen. 12:7)—is called "the glorious land." Ezekiel, following the prophets who preceded him, recognized that, because God loved "*the* land," he must necessarily purge it even as he must purge his chosen people. Thereafter Trito-Isaiah could write: "They shall raise up the former devastations" (Isa. 61:4), now that their time of "forced labor" is ended and their iniquity has been pardoned (Isa. 40:2). But now that redeemed Israel was back home in Jerusalem from exile in Babylonia, they heard God's new promise that "violence shall no more be heard in your land" (Isa. 60:18); "in your land you shall possess a double portion" (Isa. 61:7); "your land shall no more be termed Desolate; but you shall be called My delight is in her, and your land Married" (Isa. 62:4). Marvin H. Pope (*Song of Songs,* 486) suggests the order of words "honey and milk" is a reverse echo of the characterization of the Land of Promise as flowing with "milk and honey" (Exod. 3:8, 17; Lev. 20:24; Num. 13:27; Deut. 6:3). The succeeding phrase may also suggest a reversal. In Job 20:12 the evil man is pictured as storing his wickedness under his tongue in order to savor its flavor. True love seems here to have changed all that, so that it is what is good that is under her tongue.

"A garden locked . . . a fountain sealed" is evidently a lovely poetic image for a girl who has held on to her virginity. She is like the Garden of Eden before it is ravaged by the Serpent. Within it is the fountain of life: "A river flowed out of Eden to water the garden" (Gen. 2:10). Its source, of course, can be in God alone. Thus Jeremiah can complain: "They have forsaken the LORD, the fountain of living water" (Jer. 7:13). Life is evidently shut up when still in the womb of a virgin. While there it cannot create life, as a river can do in nature (Ezek. 47:1-12). Yet proleptically HE sees HER as a living tree. The meaning of *shelaḥayik* (RSV "your shoots") is difficult to determine. The root of this word is the verb "to send." Jeremiah 17:8 uses it of trees sending down roots and sending up branches. Isaiah 16:8 translates it as "branches." Then "orchard" in the RSV is actually the Persian word "paradise"; thus "a paradise of pomegranates," along with all the choicest of fruits and fragrant trees that are mentioned thereafter, may also be a pointer to the Garden of Eden. SHE is still a virgin, HE says; as such, in her beauty and fragrance she is "a garden locked, a fountain sealed."

Both HE and SHE "love" the beauties of nature. But to "love one another" as persons means a wholly different kind of loving. It was one of the tenets of the Nazi creed that the Hitler Youth should love nature. Such love leads easily to pantheism or to Baal worship (the bull god). Thus in the 20th cent. we have seen advocated the macho characteristics of the young male and the submissiveness and obedient characteristics of the sexually mature female. This teaching has led naturally, among other things, to contempt for the Jews of Germany, in that the latter portrayed before Nazi eyes the holy beauty of true love between the sexes. The worship of the human body is nature worship. Adoration of the total person is not, in that love between total persons is not a preoccupation of one's ego. HE is so fully occupied with adoration of the total HER that there is no room left in his heart for entertaining dreams of lust, of "committing adultery with her in his heart" (Matt. 5:28). By the nature of things, their love for each other is expressed in terms of Eros, but not at all in terms of Venus. Thus, despite the fact that she is still a virgin (Songs 4:12) she is potentially "a garden fountain, a well of living water" (v. 15). This is her precious possession, and it comes from God. It must not be "scattered abroad," but must be kept for "the wife of your youth," the woman you married when you were both young together (Prov. 5:15-18).

At this point, then, our editor shows how SHE has become a vehicle of revelation. A single man or a single woman can love, but separately they cannot *be* love. SHE is thus revealing that the God of the Covenant cannot be a mere monad; his ideal for her is that she should lose herself in another, as he should also. But through this her self-profession of faith in life, and by expectancy of union with her beloved who was a circumcised member of the chosen people, she was expressing a deep reality about the nature of the God of the Covenant.

The Greeks, for all their deep probing into human nature, could not have written Songs. They loved love and worshipped beauty—both of which are mere abstractions. The covenant people knew the joy of loving a *person*. When Jesus, in the true Hebraic tradition, said: "You, therefore, must be perfect" (Matt. 5:48), he was not dealing with an abstraction; for he continued, "as your heavenly Father is perfect," i.e., perfection known as the mutual love of *persons* (cf. Matt. 5:43-47). At 2 Cor. 3:17 Paul writes: "The Lord is the Spirit." The Spirit of God *creates* love. Both HE and SHE knew the Spirit—whether consciously or unconsciously does not matter—because it is within the Covenant that the Spirit is made known, so that the circumcised are enabled to respond to the Spirit's power. The mutual love of our couple was a response to the love of God.

16 The last line of Songs 4:16 is a poetic way of describing an invitation made by HER to HIM. She wishes him to "know" her in the sense we find it used at Gen. 4:1. This verb *yada'* does not describe mere carnal knowledge, or sexual intercourse. It is used with this sense of "knowing" when it describes the total knowledge that two persons have of each other when they commit themselves to each other as in the vows of marriage. We should note that the verb occurs in this sense of God and Israel at Amos 3:2: "You only have I known . . ." It is used to recognize and to accept the mystery of the other's personality. This verb, however, does not occur at Songs 4:16. In its place we have its poetic equivalent: "Let my beloved come to his garden, and eat its choicest fruits."

These lines of verse act as revelation of God's "knowledge" of his covenant people (Walther Zimmerli, *I am Yahweh,* "Knowledge of God According to the Book of Ezekiel," 29-98). The consummation of love within the Covenant is therefore not a sin. As we have seen, the canopy over the marriage bed (2:4) was what Rabbi Akiba called "the holiest of holies," a sacrosanct symbol. In consequence, in the Jewish community of Jesus' day illegitimacy was virtually unknown, whereas the covenant people of that time could describe a Gentile as "a man who had no father." Rare among the religions of the world, Judaism has retained what we call a woman's right to—and need for—sexual satisfaction.

SHE is clearly aware of the potential life within her, a life that must remain captive till it is released by her lover. We recall that the name Eve probably means "life-giver." It is God's will, she knows in her innocence, that this should be so; for it was in the Garden that God had said: ". . . and they became *one flesh.* And the man and his wife (or "his woman") were both naked, and were not ashamed" (Gen. 2:24-25). She calls upon the forces of nature, which are one with her own physical body, to induce her beloved to come to her. Thereupon he becomes one flesh with her, without any inhibitions but in fullness of joy. For, as Gen. 2:23 puts it: He exclaims, "This *at last* is bone of my bones and flesh of my flesh."

CHAPTER 5

1 HE obeys her call: "I have entered my garden," he says. So their union has now been consummated. With that he has found that oneness with his beloved in sexual embrace is indeed "very heaven." This is expressed by his describing the experience in terms of the delicacies mentioned above, since they were accepted as food of the gods. We read: "I came, I gathered, I ate, I drank." His experience was thus a kind of divine banquet set forth for them both by a loving God.

So the chorus sings: "Eat, our friends, and drink to the full, you lovers!" (author's translation). The chorus, who are aware of the source of covenant love, agrees that their joy in each other comes from God himself—although this is not stated.

2-8 This independent poem expresses in fascinating language the agony and the ecstasy of love. "I slept" does not express a once-only experience, but, as a participle, suggests that her experience is one SHE dreams about night after night: "my heart was awake." She half dreams, half imagines her beloved knocking at the door, his head "wet with dew." The wording "my locks with the drops of the night" reveals a good guess at the meaning on the part of the RSV, in that the word translated "locks" occurs only in this chapter of Songs. Some commentators note sexual overtones in both sections of v. 3, but this need not be so. For example, a straightforward interpretation of v. 3 would be that the girl had gone to bed. Thus, before she could open the door she would have to soil her feet once again on the earthen floor, as she groped for her dress. She would have preferred to welcome her beloved without mud between her toes! But the longing of her heart was answered without her aid. HE opened the door himself and entered, and came to her in her cleanliness of both body and soul.

A dream cannot be analyzed with logical exactitude; it often includes irrelevant details. Verse 5 is certainly ecstatically poetic before it is even descriptive. But dreams contain unknown horrors and setbacks. Such a contretemps is vividly expressed now in dream terms in v. 7, revealing that her unconscious mind is deeply troubled by the "agony" of love. Yet, the chorus is also present in her dream, to the extent that she can address them as friends and neighbors, no matter whether "in heaven" or "on earth."

A phrase occurs in v. 4 that we should question. It is the RSV rendering "my heart was thrilled within me." The NEB is closer to the Hebrew with "my bowels," really meaning "all my innards," for these were all supposed to be seats of various emotions. But we are in the area of "the agony and the ecstacy" here. The line really reads: "My innards grew hot within me." Jeremiah, in agony of spirit, had to exclaim, "My anguish, my anguish! I writhe in pain" (Jer. 4:19 RSV), "anguish" being this same word "innards." The same is said of God. At Isa. 16:11 we hear, literally: "Therefore my innards grew hot for Moab," as the prophet expresses his anguish at Moab's fate. We shall note later that such anguish is part and parcel of the love of God. What particular anguish then, is SHE experiencing in these terrible nightmares?

9 The chorus, aware of her heartrending experience, and in their living concern for her, thereupon ask her as she springs awake from her bed: Why do you suppose that "your beloved (is) more than another beloved," in that you charge us with the task of looking for him? If and when we find him, do you really want us to tell him that you love him to distraction?

10-16 HER reply comes in a beautiful poem, showing why her beloved is indeed "more than any other." Yet, of course, these words could be spoken by any lover about his or her beloved. The point is that SHE had in fact chosen HIM, just as HE had chosen HER. Each had done so, because with the eyes of love the beloved appears to be perfection itself. He is, she says: "distinguished among ten thousand." Thus, as individual members within that one people who had been chosen by God—on the ground only that he loved them (Deut. 4:37)—they discover that, possessing such love in their mutual relationship, they had received it from God himself.

According to Songs 5:10, "My beloved is all radiant," i.e., his face shines with love. This is what happens to a young man when he is in communion with his beloved. He can be compared to Moses, whose face shone when he came down from Mt. Sinai after communing with the God of love (Exod. 34:29). Moreover, HE is "ruddy." The Hebrew word is "red," thus the meaning may go be-

yond "ruddy." Being "radiant" from love, his emotions would be
heightened, and he might well have been red-faced from excitement
and joy. Or again, like the young David, he could have looked ruddy
from health or "wholeness," such as comes from possessing deep
satisfaction.

"Locks" is the rare word we noted at Songs 5:2. "Fitly set," as the
RSV margin admits, is only a guess. Literally the words mean "(his
eyes) sit in fulness." Did the "springs of water" fill a container of
some description that was used to irrigate the family vineyard and
provide water for the domestic animals? "His palate" (RSV "his
speech"), and so perhaps "his kisses" are "most sweet" (v. 16). "Set
with (or "full of") jewels" (v. 14) could express a double entendre
such as Hebrew poetry delighted in. "Jewels" is the Hebrew word
Tarshish, the name of a city away to the west; for if this city was really Tartessus in Spain, it would be an entrepôt for the spoils of West
Africa (cf. Jonah 1:3). The ships that made this lengthy and adven-
turous voyage were known as ships of Tarshish, the name coming to
be applied to any large vessel capable of voyaging far. In the same
way the 19th cent. spoke of Atlantic liners, even if these plowed the
Indian Ocean. So "tarshish" could be either the precious cargo these
ships carried or the name could describe their powerful and swift
movement through the seas.

The main point to note is that SHE describes HIM in language
comparable to HIS language about HER in Songs 4:1-8. Neither is
more beautiful than the other. Because of their love for each other
they are equally lovely in the sight of God and mankind. So she can
conclude as she answers the question of the chorus (v. 16): "He is
altogether desirable. That is how you will recognize my beloved, O
daughters of Jerusalem" (author's translation).

CHAPTER 6

1 The chorus replies once again, having heard this description of the young lover: "Where are we to seek him with you?" The women of the chorus are concerned for her in love and seek her good. Here again love has elicited love.

2-3 SHE replies in a manner that is surely logical but is full of the delights of poetry. "He has gone down to his garden to be with me, to delight in me and to 'gather lilies.'" She sums this up in the words: "I am my beloved's and my beloved is mine." There is no shame in their love for each other (cf. Gen. 2:25); they only wish the "daughters of Jerusalem" to know that in each other they have found that peace which passes all understanding. Songs is reticent to use theological language. It consistently remains in the sphere of human experience. It does not say that such peace comes from the God of peace. Yet Songs 6:3a is an echo of God's declaration to Israel when he bestowed his Covenant upon them (Hos. 2:19-20, 23; Jer. 31:3, 34; Ezek. 24:25). To this lovely vision here, then, we must remember to add also that throughout the OT work in a garden or in a vineyard seems to symbolize God's plan of a healthy creative life for both men and women. As the philosopher Thomas Carlyle put it: "Work such as this is a sacrament of communion with the Highest."

There are literalistic and moralistic persons who ask the question anxiously: "Why is there no mention at any point in Songs of the young couple getting married to each other?" Such persons do not recognize that the OT is a book about God and his plan for the redemption of the world, and not about morality or the mere history of the people of Israel. What Songs offers us in our various human cultures is a revelation of the love of God, as we shall see later, which is why it makes no attempt to write a prosaic biography of events in the life of a human couple in love.

4-10 Following is another love poem that HE utters in praise of HER. This clearly is no speech of a lascivious Solomon.

31

It seems odd to compare a woman's beauty with that of a city. The RSV has kept the name, Tirzah, a city that may have disappeared by postexilic times. It is mentioned in Josh. 12:24 and 1 Kgs. 14:17, and again in 1 Kgs. 15 and 16. But the word derives from a root meaning "pleasantness." Probably the name alluded to something meaningful to the hearer at the time, but which is lost to us today.

"Terrible as an army with banners": if this army were approaching you, you would indeed be afraid. It seems that he finds her so disturbing that he has to beg her to turn her eyes away. The word "terrible," however, is used elsewhere in the sense of horrifying, awe-inspiring, especially of a theophany, of God manifesting himself to human consciousness. See the description of such a theophany at Hab. 3:3-15. What HE is experiencing is his share of agony in love that goes with the ecstasy. SHE had experienced it in a series of nightmares (Songs 5:2-7). HIS is the more awesome path for a man to tread. Suddenly he is discovering, as we all must, that love is not all unruffled pleasure. Looking into her eyes, the eyes of a woman made in the image of God, he becomes aware of the deep mystery of human life and human love. True love—as he knows theirs to be—must, it seems, contain within it the mystery of suffering. Made in God's image, both HE and SHE must make the new beginning together, plumbing the ultimate reality of the love of God.

Such thoughts had not as yet entered his mind. But now, by the providence of God, he must face this issue. Suddenly he has glimpsed this ultimate reality in the look his beloved gave him. He is not as yet able to bear the cup of suffering that is altogether bound up with love, and he has to beg her to avert her eyes from his. Only then can he, lightheartedly, continue with his adulation of her beauty. He does so in language that may have been common to the poets, as it has occurred already at 4:1-2.

8-10   These verses may be a snatch of a separate poem, or they may be what follows from the terrible experience HE has just narrated. The reference is not specifically to Solomon. The NEB expresses it better: Suppose the case of a king having sixty queens and eighty concubines and maidens without number. What would he ever know of love? He assumed that intercourse with a beautiful woman—not when she wished it, but when he demanded it—was all that sexual union could offer. A moment's passion, and then forgotten. But our young man now saw things otherwise. The Baals of the Canaanites had always "possessed" many concubines. According to the prophet Hosea, God's chosen people (Hos. 3:2) had gone off in his day to fornicate with the Baals in the sense to which our poem is pointing. In taking Israel home, however, as Hos. 2:16 puts it, the LORD had declared that she would no longer think of him as "Baal" (for that word also means "lord"), for a Baal has many wives. Rather, Israel would call the LORD *ishi*, "my husband," my one-and-only-man. For by God's grace she will have come to know the meaning of true conjugal love. Thereafter, all the prophets after Hosea accepted the fact that Israel was Yahweh's one and only Bride.

The poem goes on. SHE is not a lone individual cast on the goodwill of a generous state, as she might be in the Western world today. In fact, the West seems to think that such should be the norm for society, since the society of the West takes casual sex also as the norm. She may "shack up" with a man for a time, speak of a common-law marriage that lasts for a month or two, and then dissolve the partnership, each being tired of the other . . . but the woman may be left with an unwanted baby. No, our SHE lives in a happy home, where she is the only daughter of her mother, and a full member of the extended family of the village community. The RSV's reading, "darling," is actually the word "one," "unique." That is why it translates by "darling"! Not only does HE think HER to be flawless, "pure," so does her mother! (cf. Songs 5:2). We see then that the mother accepts her daughter's intimacy with her young man as being good and true, in no sense immoral, but in accordance with the plan of God for the covenant people.

It is interesting that this mother's beloved daughter is praised for her moral purity by such "sex experts" as the chorus seems to be. They refer to her purity perhaps with envy, and then repeat the line we examined at 6:4 ("terrible as an army with banners"). It would seem that they are discovering that their sensual existence is being judged by the purity of our beloved daughter's life and attitude to the whole issue of sex. Our young woman's life is a form of preaching about the love of God. "Who is this?" they exclaim, in wonder that any woman should remain uncontaminated by the filth that too often goes along with human sexuality. "*Bright* as the sun" employs the Hebrew word *barah,* which was translated "flawless" in the previous verse. But the "sun" here is not the usual word *shemesh,* but the term *ha-hammah.* This is a poetic term meaning "the heat." One wonders if it has been chosen deliberately to relate to the idea of the heat of the love of God (v. 4; cf. Deut. 4:15; Isa. 33:14).

Human life is lived out on a knife-edge, and a person can remain thereon only by the grace of God. There is no neutrality in this war

that we must wage daily. In speaking of this "knife-edge," Deuteronomy 30:15 says: "See, I have set before you this day life and good,
death and evil." Sex is a basic element in our human constitution. In
obedience to God it can be the instrument of God's blessing, a blessing that conveys joy, exultation, and *shalom*. If handled in disobedience, its violent force can be terrible as an army with "banners," in
which case it can lead through war within oneself from lust to misery, and from misery to very hell.

11-12 Here is a "snippet" of what may have been a longer poem.
SHE speaks again, telling us (1) of his love of nature, and (2) of his
practical interest in his plantation. It seems that a wadi cut through
the vineyard, a riverbed along which a torrent might rush in winter,
but only a trickle in a dry summer. The vinegrower had to watch his
water supply carefully, even though both fruit trees and vines de-
pend more on deep-level sources of water than on a surface flow. It
seems that SHE carries a vision of him in her mind as she goes about
her work as a member of a family of viticulturalists or grape growers.
The NEB translates: "to look at the rushes by the stream," but this
is merely another way of referring to the irrigating of the vineyard.
The word translated "rushes" occurs only once again, at Job 8:11,
so that that may not be the definitive translation.

"I did not know myself," the Hebrew continues; "placed me . . .
the chariots of my people." These words, probably now a corrupt
rendering of a lost original, have produced many attempts at making
sense of them. The LXX is virtually meaningless. The KJV (AV)
has: "Or ever I was aware, my soul made me like the chariots of
Amminadib," or, in the margin, "set me on the chariots of my
willing people." The NEB has: "She [?] made me feel more than a
prince reigning over the myriads of his people." TEV, again, is quite
different: "I am trembling [that is, "not aware of myself"]; you have
me as eager for love as a chariot driver is for battle." The broken text
probably means something like: "Before I realized it (the longing)
in my soul had seated me on a chariot with him whom my people
regarded as noble." The exact meaning is now beyond recovery.
What the sentence seems to be saying is that her mind was not on
her task; rather, in imagination she was riding on a chariot with her
beloved.

13 The chorus has seen him galloping off, so to speak, in her imagination, with HER in his chariot, and cries to her, "Come back,
come back." They cry out: "O Shulammite." This word actually oc-

curs twice in this verse. In this wild runaway with her "prince" SHE feels that he is a real prince, in a sense that Solomon in all his glory knew nothing about.

The name "Shulammite" derives from the Hebrew root *sh-l-m*, from which we get the noun *shalom*, meaning "peace." Solomon's name also comes from this root. *Shulammith* is simply a possible feminine form of Solomon, one that becomes Salome in Greek. There is no reason to adopt other interpretations of these lines, some of which connect the cry of the chorus with the activities of Solomon in Songs 1, while, of course, others read into it aspects of Canaanite mythology. In so doing they regard the name as a feminine form of *Shelem*, who was the moon-goddess Ishtar, the sex symbol of the Canaanite high places; or, as William Foxwell Albright suggested, she was the goddess Anath, whose blood-thirsty dance is vividly portrayed in the Anath episode of the Baal epic. No, the chorus is so enamoured of her that they want to recall her from her daydream "that we may gaze upon you, as you dance with joy in the vineyard."

We all love to see a young girl exulting in what is the greatest thing in the world, love. SHE "twists," says the Hebrew (unwittingly using the same term as the name of a modern dance), between two rows of vines, overwhelmed and exulting in the thrill of her love for HIM. The vines sway and bow in sympathy with her, as if they were joining in the "dance of the two camps," perhaps something like the old English dance we know as "The Grand Old Duke of York."

CHAPTER 7

1-5 The editor places a new and separate poem at this point to balance HER admiration for HIM with a vivid description of HIS admiration for HER. His words are the sentiments of poets everywhere. When he calls to her "O queenly maiden!" he is probably only regarding her as his own "queen," and is making no reference to Solomon's harem. The very explicit description of physical beauty in this poem is to be evaluated not by modern Western standards but against its oriental background, for there are non-Western cultures in today's world that are not in line with Western standards of judgment. Anyway, at this point in the ordering of the poems the theme clearly relates to married love.

The geographical reference in v. 4 is beyond our grasp to envision. Heshbon was a royal city of the Amorites; it is mentioned in Num. 21:25-34. Today it lies in the present kingdom of Jordan. Such cities necessarily had pools or reservoirs within their walls, and this city would have gates such as the one named here. But as to why that particular city was picked upon for mention we do not know. "Your nose" in Songs 7:4 could alternatively mean "your face." TEV renders v. 5 by "Your head is held high like Mount Carmel." Carmel is that isolated peak which looks down upon today's city of Haifa. It is the first higher ground to receive the rain-bearing winds that blow from the southwest over the Mediterranean Sea, so that Carmel is better watered than are the plains. But, curiously, we might connect the last two references by learning from Franz Delitzsch that in modern Arabic Carmel is known as the "nose of the mountain-range" (*The Song of Songs,* 127). (See 1 Kgs. 18:41-45.)

"A king is held captive . . ." could be rendered, "Any king would be held captive—how much more am I, your one and only lover?" "Tresses"; just as water flowing into a trough (such as was filled by the trickle from the wadi suggested at Songs 6:11) twists and curls (Hebrew *rahat*), so do her tresses.

6-9 This is another and separate love poem sung by HIM, though

36

some regard it as being all one with vv. 1-5. The important point to note is that each, both HE and SHE, loves the other equally, neither of them dominating the other. At v. 6 the RSV margin quotes the Hebrew literally, "in delights." Some commentators read an erotic connotation into v. 8. But others point out that the only way one can harvest dates is to climb the date palm!

10-13 This again is a separate poem, where SHE is the speaker. It begins with a strong statement that *agape* and *eros,* spiritual and physical love, cannot be separated from each other, as they are in Greek thought. The OT does not separate them any more than it would think of separating body from soul. What we read is: "I belong to my beloved, and his physical longing is upon me." The Hebrew reader would actually concretize this statement of HERS because he would recognize an overtone in the word *teshuqah,* "desire." Its root, *shuq,* can also mean the "thigh." The noun used is that which we find at Gen. 3:16, but employed here in a new and loving sense.

Knowing that HE has fallen in love with HER, she urges him to take her into the countryside to visit the family vineyards and orchard. (Note that Songs 7:12d occurs also at 6:11d.) "There I will give you my love." The LXX has "There I will give you my breasts," meaning "There we shall consummate our love."

13 The mandrake plant, in ancient Near Eastern mythology, was connected with fertility and with the love-goddess, whose name varied from country to country. Clearly SHE has no objection to "adopting" the ideas connected with it. In the OT the object of marriage was fruitfulness, the bearing of children. We moderns, blessed with all the advantages of modern medical science, find it difficult to remember that perhaps five out of every six babies born to a family in the ancient world might die at birth or in infancy. By pointing to the mandrakes that she had "laid up" for her beloved (isn't she sly?), she is virtually saying to him: "Because I am a member of the chosen people, I dare to say: 'May the fruit of our union in our total passionate love for each other result in the birth of a baby.'" The theological significance of this we shall examine later.

CHAPTER 8

1-4 That this is a love poem and not a report on an actual situation is borne out by the change of address from "brother" to "lover," although the latter word is not present here. Then there is a change to the chorus. They, this time, are evidently watching the young couple's lovemaking as if from the point of view of eternity, and SHE addresses them as if in prayer. SHE wishes that as lovers they might have a little more privacy. If HE had been her brother, then, as brother and sister they could have met in the street and she could have greeted him with a sisterly kiss without the tongue-wagging that fills the day for idle watchers. If he were her brother, she would naturally have brought him into her home. There her mother would have received them in love. It was her mother, she says, who had taught her all she knew (about sex and lovemaking?). That is one possible rendering; the RSV is conjectural. The NEB footnote offers another possible reading: "for you to teach me how to love you."

It seems that the villagers where they lived were rather straitlaced (not like the people of the royal court!) in their ideas. For lovers to kiss on the street simply was not "done." There are cultures in the world today that would fully understand and appreciate such a regulation. We have only to think of the Arab world.

But he is not my brother. He is my beloved! O how I wish we were even now making love together.

She turns to the heavenly choir, figured as "the daughters of Jerusalem" (remember, for our editor, there was no separation between heaven and earth), to leave her and her beloved in peace—either, with the NEB margin, "while she is resting" (which would make HIM the speaker) or until the moment for lovemaking comes naturally.

5 This is a one-line question sung by the choir that leads into the situation where HE utters, in a separate song, the remainder of our v. 5.

5b All true lovers become overwhelmed at times as they contemplate the mysteries of love and of birth and human life. HE suggests that he found his beloved asleep under an apple tree, probably in her family orchard. What strikes him is that, as either SHE or her mother must have told him, it was there that his beloved's mother had first felt the oncoming of birth pains; she would then have been helped into the house and made comfortable. It is only too easy for a couple in love to be so bound up in love for each other that they ignore the relationship of their mutual love to the ongoing life of the world. It is noteworthy that while Gen. 1:26 refers to humanity as *adam*—as one, male and female together—*adam* can also mean the male. But the word for female is not that word in its feminine form, *adamah*. "The female" is known instead by her specialized function, *hawwah*, Eve, meaning "life-producer" (Gen. 3:20). Our couple now become deeply aware of this.

The realization of this mystery now sweeps over HIM, namely that their love affair now comes in a succession leading back from generation to generation. He had heard the Torah being read in the synagogue (if the synagogue may be dated so early) on the sabbath. So now there flashes into his mind the significance of the many "begats" he had heard read out from it. Genesis 5 reads: "This is the book of the generations of Adam" (RSV). "When God created human beings, he made them like himself. He created them male and female . . ." (TEV). "When Enosh had lived ninety years, he became the father of Kenan . . . and he died . . ." (RSV). So our young man, by a "hint" from God, as the Lord wandered in the orchard, was able to see his love affair in perspective. HIS love for HER was of God, for he had created them both for this. The first pair of human beings had met and loved in a garden of fruit trees, and had become parents themselves *with* the LORD, as the Hebrew puts it at Gen. 4:1. The wonder and mystery of the continuity of mankind was being opened up to HIM. Conception and travail were not new (cf. Ps. 139:13-16), though this fact of human life was now being experienced by both him and his beloved. They were, in fact, entering into the long line of the procreation of mankind, something that was always accomplished through pain, yet of God himself. Accordingly, the fruit of their lovemaking would be the arrival of a baby to continue the succession of mankind.

In this way all human life is naturally orientated toward the future, in hope. If this is true of a simple young couple, it is true of all history, in that they as parents are history itself. History is meaningful now as a process that is creating the future of eternity, *now* (cf.

Matt. 25:40). So even our present broken history *matters,* i.e., events cannot be abstracted from their actual consequences (cohabitation produces conception and a new generation!). "An event is not what it is in itself, but what it is in its actual context and in terms of the future it anticipates" (Wolfhart Pannenberg).

6-7 The following passage, perhaps the greatest hymn to love ever expressed, was uttered, we should note, by a woman. In the same way, among the love letters of Abelard and Eloise (she died A.D. 1142), hers are the most moving expressions of love in the whole medieval period.

The word for "seal" describes an amulet worn either round the neck (Gen. 38:18) or as a ring on the hand (Gen. 41:42; Jer. 22:24). Thus it could be quickly unfastened and used to seal a document. SHE does not ask HIM for an engagement ring to be placed on the fourth finger of her left hand, as a modern woman would expect from her beloved. She asks him to take her herself into his very heart, and make *her* the seal of their love. The seal revealed that their promise of love to each other was "for ever." (The word "arm" in Hebrew can be used loosely for "hand.") At Deut. 6:4-9 is preserved what might be called Israel's basic "creed." It begins: "Hear, O Israel: the LORD our God is one LORD: and you shall love. . . ." That is, as a sign of the total commitment in love of its "heart, soul, and might," Israel was to "bind" the words of this creed "as a sign upon your hand." The love of which Deut. 6 speaks is total love, total commitment, right unto death. Not only so, but love comes even before a person's faith in God, yet not before God's faith in that person. If the churches of the world would but recognize this, there would be fewer ecclesiastical quarrels about matters of belief. That creed was given to Israel by God, and ever since—even to this day—has been regarded by Israel as the basis of its very existence, its raison d'être. In our present Song the emphasis of this creed is now developed. Death is strong, meaning that it prevails over all humanity; that is, all people, both male and female, must necessarily die. But love is just as strong as is death, and this is because *love is life*! This is because love is a power that comes, not from our human constitution, but from God, the living God, the God who created both life and death. The word translated by "vehement flame" in the RSV is really "flame of God." Some take it to be a superlative, meaning something like an "almighty great flame." But there is no reason why it may not be understood literally as it is written. If so, it would be declaring that the kind of love spoken of here is beyond the human mind to interpret, for it has its source in the God of love that is both passionate and devouring (cf. Isa. 33:14).

What modern, Western mankind must seek to grasp, if it has been weaned on the "Greek" view of reality, is that death can come upon us *now* if we reject love, and not merely after we are laid in the grave. New life from God may grasp us *now,* and in consequence be unaffected by physical death. Jesus did not declare a new thing when he said: "Leave the dead to bury their own dead" (Luke 9:60). He was only rendering explicit that which is the faith of the OT prophets and of the editor of Songs.

It is a pity that the modern English word "jealousy" does not mean what it means in Hebrew. As in the case of all "biblical language," we are to take into account that the languages of mankind, created by sinful human beings, are not capable of interpreting what is the nature of God himself.

The idea of Hebrew *qin'ah,* "jealousy," is inherent in the concept of the election of Israel. Since human language is not adequate to convey the "thoughts" of God, these thoughts are conveyed to us in pictures, on a level that the human mind can "see." This, of course, is the method of Jesus' teaching when he declared: "The kingdom of heaven is *like* treasure hidden in a field . . ." (Matt. 13:44).

Beginning with Hosea, certain of the prophets likened God's election of Israel to his "choice" of one people, and one only, chosen to be his Bride ever since the days of Moses. While God loved all mankind, he chose to love Israel in a special way (Deut. 4:32-40). To this end he made a Covenant with her, with the words "I will be your God, and you shall be my people." Such love was not a display of favoritism, as Deuteronomy emphasizes. Israel was chosen by God to serve God, not to boast that there was something special about her that had attracted God's attention. Why God had chosen Israel was a divine mystery. Among much else he had chosen to "discipline them," and to that end "he let you see his great fire" (Deut. 4:36). After Israel had lived within the covenant for hundreds of years, but still had not learned *why* God had chosen her, the prophet Amos felt bound to speak for God as follows: "You only have I known (in the sense of the intimacy of marriage) of all the families of the earth; therefore I will punish you . . ." (Amos 3:2). God's passionate love is as implacable (Hebrew *qashah*) as the grave, as Sheol, the place of the dead. His love is all-demanding. He seeks to receive back from his Bride the total self-giving that he himself gives. Anything else would be merely "love" as the world knows it, sexual passion that soon melts away. Thus the total love of God as he gave himself to his Bride, Israel, is his "jealous" love, a word that takes its place naturally in the Decalogue, where, in the Second Commandment (Exod. 20:4), God's command to Israel to love him alone is expounded in detail. Israel was to have no other lovers. No male god dare cuckold (or deceive) the living God, as Hosea warned Israel in dramatic picture language. A true Husband and Lover is overwhelmingly jealous for the Bride he has chosen, elected, out of all the other possible candidates whom he meets in the course of his daily pursuits.

Unaware of this biblical realism, many people in the West, in this permissive age, cannot understand why sex relations require that "love" be set in the context of history, or in the perspective of a divine plan working through the story of humanity. The result is that the West has produced a "now" generation that has little interest in its past history; in fact, many young people, unsettled and restless, may even be unaware of who their grandparents are. In consequence, this "now" generation looks at the Christian faith in a self-centered and selfish light. Countless young people are concerned only about their own personal religious experience, and may even claim to be "born again" Christians—yet the while thinking nothing of divorce or of men and women living together in temporary relationships. Such *"now"* Christians are usually unable to recognize that both Jews and Christians in the *"new"* churches of the Third World regard them with pity.

Not only is the love of God "jealous," it is a "great fire" (Deut. 4:36). In fact, it is frequently described in terms of heat, so that the word *qin'ah* can be translated not only by "jealousy" but also by "passion." God may be "furiously angry," even passionately so (TEV), if a third party seeks to woo away his beloved; the Hebrew words *harah, 'ashan, qatsaph* are all used to convey this reality in picture terms (one such is, literally, "his nose grew hot"! e.g., Exod. 4:14; 32:11). It is at our peril that we—in our 20th cent. "enlightened" view of God, or under the influence of the Eastern religions—reject the concept of God's wrath that is pictured for us in terms of fire in both the OT and NT (Matt. 3:11; 7:19; 2 Thess. 1:7-8; Rev. 20:14). Such then, declares this poem, is the nature of true love.

7   "Many waters" are spoken of frequently in the OT, and as well are referred to in the NT (Rev. 17:1). These are again expressed pictorially, as the forces of evil that surge up from the depths of the earth, from the *tehom,* the ocean of chaos (Gen. 1:2), which has been

there from the beginning of creation. "The water under the earth" is referred to in the Second Commandment (Exod. 20:4). The Psalms frequently speak of these waters as being powerless before the creative plan of the love of God, e.g., Ps. 46:3. "Love lies beyond the tomb," as the 19th cent. poet, John Clare, puts it. That is to say, the threat from and the power of the waters are irrelevant where love is, for love is of God. As Isa. 43:2 puts it: "When you pass through the waters I will be with you." God does not remove the waters. Mankind must necessarily face the power of the "many waters." For most of us today in Western society, these are the overwhelmingly strong attractions of a consumer society. Yet these are powerless to drown love. They cannot "quench" it, the word used for putting out a fire. This is because it is "not of this world." Love belongs in a different sphere from the "floods." That is why believing, loving people scorn those who imagine that love can be purchased (as Solomon supposed) by those "things" that belong in the same sphere as the "floods."

8-10 Our editor is a good theologian. It is at this point in the development of his thesis that he includes a poem which contributes to and expands upon the picture of true love that he has compiled step by step. The contents of this poem supplement and complete the meaning of love he is seeking to express.

Though SHE is the speaker, no longer can she say "I"; this is because she now shares her life with her husband. And though HE is not related to his beloved's "little sister," SHE speaks as if this younger girl belonged to them both now that they are "one."

Too often we hear the quip: "Two's company, three's none" (or "three's a crowd"). And it is of course possible for a couple to be so immersed in each other that they have no time for others. Their two-way love is actually just selfishness multiplied by two. The couple in our poem had gone through that phase (Songs 3:5; 8:4). By now however, as we have seen, SHE has led her beloved to look in love and compassion on a third party. She sings: "We have [not, "I have"] a little sister." This little sister is still too young to know the joy, excitement, and peace that you and I have discovered together in true love, she means. So there rises in her heart a proper concern for the sister who has not yet reached her teens. "What shall we do for our sister?"

The OT has little to say about friendship, for it can be exclusive of any third party, though it has much to say about loyalty. This reality is hidden within the noun *hesed. Hesed* is a covenant term, the supreme covenant term, in fact. In OT usage it binds together those who are in covenant with each other. This meaning of the word was not recognized actually till the 20th cent. A concordance will show that it has been translated in many ways by such terms as "favor," "mercy," "grace," "beauty," "kindness," "love," "loving-kindness," and more. But here we are witnessing HER family loyalty.

The symbolism of the answer she herself gives has produced many interpretations. In light of the prevailing symbolism of the previous poems, however, it would seem that "wall" and "door" are to be understood as parallel pictures. "Since little sister is still a virgin," she is saying, "her hand having not yet been asked in marriage, she is inviolate, and we shall do all in our power to keep her so." This promise is expressed in two ways for emphasis. It is a terrible thing to violate or rape a girl. Rape takes for granted a dualistic view of human nature, that the "soul" is something apart from the "body." "I was once like her," she declares, "but my breasts soon developed to be like towers. Only *then* (emphatic) have I become and now am (*hayiti*) in his eyes a woman who could bring him peace, *shalom*, wholeness of being, by growing into perfect union with him. If we had had sexual relations before I was mature we would have missed out on the real joy of mutual love."

11-12 The editor selects a little poem he has at his command to end his collections of songs, one that answers the manner in which his selection began. It began (ch. 1) with the person of Solomon as its hero, the poor-rich man who had missed out on the greatest thing in the world. Now here, our proper hero points out that Solomon had a vineyard at Baal-hamon. The editor's choice of terms is to be noted. First, our lover's beloved belonged to a family that owned a vineyard. This homely market garden had turned out to be a veritable Garden of Eden. As Robert Browning wrote: "I always see the garden and God there a-making man's wife" (*Fra Lippo Lippi*, 265).

Second, at Isa. 5:1-7 we read, God speaking: "Let me sing for my beloved a love song concerning his vineyard." The last verse (Isa. 5:7) runs: "For the vineyard of the LORD of hosts is the house of Israel." The passage then concludes with these harsh-sounding words: "He looked for justice (*mishpat*), but behold, bloodshed (*mispah*); for righteousness (*tsedaqah*), but behold, a cry (*tse'aqah*)!" The vineyard that Israel was was evidently no longer the home of love. What then, third, about Solomon's vineyard? The one in Baal-hamon? We note that the first words in the Hebrew text of Songs 8:11 are identical with those at Isa. 5:1b.

Baal was, of course, the Canaanite god of growth and fertility. There were many Baals in the Levant, each with a different manifestation, a different theological significance. The worship of some of them was merely an excuse for licentious behavior by both sexes, as Hosea makes plain. Some Greeks identified Baal with Heracles (Hercules), the champion who became a god after performing twelve great labors. So virile was he, as we noted before, that he was supposed to have impregnated seventy women in one night. Hebrew *hamon* means two things, "wealth" and "a crowd, a multitude"; so the poem employs figurative language to show not where, but what kind of a vineyard Solomon had—it was in fact a sumptuous harem. To let out the vineyard to keepers may possibly mean that Solomon found his wives and concubines too many even for him to handle. So he allowed the richest members of his court to sport with some of his wives—at a price. An aspect of this possibility we find in 1 Kgs. 11:1-8. There we learn that these women worshipped innumerable foreign gods in licentious rites.

If this is so, then Songs 8:12 speaks for itself. Solomon may have one thousand females as his share, the rich fornicators two hundred each—"for all I care," HE means. But "my vineyard, my very own, is for myself." True love can dwell only in the home where monogamous marriage is held in honor.

13 This little verse, spoken by the chorus, is addressed to the couple who dwell in their garden of love. It employs both masculine and feminine forms, as if it were inviting each of the two equally to describe the *shalom* they now enjoy, overshadowed as they now are by the watchful presence of the chorus. SHE expresses for the world to hear her desire for a love set free of all Canaanite concepts, what a true love within the covenant of God's love in his relationship with Israel means for one of God's children.

14 SHE does so by letting them overhear her invitation to her beloved to come to her side. HE, meanwhile, is in the very "seventh heaven," "up in the clouds"—the language used by such a prophet as Habakkuk. The last verses of the latter's poem (Hab. 3:18-19) describe exaltation of spirit and of "joying in the God of my salvation," as when "he makes my feet like hinds' feet, he makes me tread upon the tops of the mountains." And have we not seen that such love belongs in eternity?

THEOLOGICAL IMPLICATIONS

1. We have noted that the Song of Songs is not a chance collection of love poems. Their editor has evidently made a selection for his purpose from an anthology of poems that may well have been recited at village weddings. But, if they had been so used, then they were recited at random by the village bard. Our editor, in making his selection, has placed them in an order that, as we can see now, goes according to an ascending plan. He was an Israelite, the heir of the revelation God had given Israel through Moses at Sinai. He was aware that he belonged to the chosen people, a reality assured to him because he had been circumcised. Thus he had come to discover something of the nature and purpose of God, the God of the Covenant. He had come to recognize that the work of the great preexilic prophets, as they interpreted and applied their Mosaic heritage, had by now been accepted as Holy Scripture.

More than all, he had discovered by just living his life together with his wife and family that, their having been created in the image of God, the love that held this family together and gave it meaning could only be a gift from God. For the love experienced within the covenant of his marriage depended upon the love of God given to Israel through his Covenant, of which the Gentiles knew scarcely anything.

He was aware, with the prophet Hosea, that God always acts first in his dealing with human beings, before the human is able to make any response. Yet our editor also recognized, conversely, that the human's response, under God, can reveal—or at least point to—aspects of the nature of God. With this in mind, he has so placed together, in the order we have them now, the poems of his peasant people that they reveal—and do so to this day—the ultimate reality that God is love.

2. In Songs 1:1-7 the editor introduces us to the inadequate concept of love held by all hedonists, citing King Solomon as typical of those who suppose that unredeemed, egotistical, and self-centered men and women can ever discover what true love is like.

46

The series of poems have been set in an ascending order of significance (cf. 1 Cor. 12:31b), leading virtually to what we would dare to describe as "revelation."

a. The kind of "love" that Solomon displays, as *ba'al* of his harem, is merely sexual attraction or even just "the lust of the eye."

b. So the editor turns to a sincere young couple who meet and fall in love. At first this "love" looks like "calf love," in that they have not yet met with the realities of life, the new kind of life into which they are just about to enter.

c. They discover that true love must experience both the agony and the ecstasy. True love must be jealous, in the sense that it excludes all others. It is what Hosea speaks of when he declares to Israel: "In that day . . .you will call me, 'My husband' (*ish*) [in the "one-man, one-woman relationship"], and no longer will you call me, 'my Ba'al' [the title for the male head of a harem of females]."

d. True love calls forth total commitment to each other, one male, one female, who find when they consummate their love that they have entered into a wholly new relationship.

e. This new relationship is creative through pain and travail. It includes the creative exploration of each other's personalities, and this in turn reveals that their relationship is not complete without a concern in love for a third party.

f. Such total love is evidently "not of this world." It is as strong as death. It is *le-'olam, "into* eternity"; and it "embodies" for unsophisticated human beings what the NT describes as "the joy of the LORD."

3. When Jesus declared: "Blessed are the poor," he was not saying, "Blessed are the deprived, the hungry, the destitute." He was speaking, rather, of the *'am haarets,* the "people of the land," the rather despised peasantry who had little chance to know either Torah or the polite ways of the upper classes in Jerusalem. In other words, Jesus was saying, "Blessed are the unsophisticated."

Our poems thus move from the sophisticated atmosphere of the royal court to the simple, plain life of ordinary Israelites who had to earn their living by the sweat of their brow. Thus in our poems there appears an ordinary peasant lad who has fallen in love with an ordinary peasant girl. She is not a mere unit in herself, however, for she belongs to a loving, caring family and community. By his selection of poems our editor shows that HE comes to adore HER to the same extent as SHE adores HIM. We see this mutuality and equality when they express their love for each other in parallel terms.

In the early period of the development of the Hebrew language, the one word *ha'* stood for both *he* and *she*. Later these two pronouns were differentiated: the masculine *ha'* was written as *hu'*, while the feminine was written as *hi'*. (At what point in history the development was made we cannot say, as the whole text of the OT was edited about the time of the editing of Songs.) In other words, the original pronoun that could be recited as *he* could equally well be recited as *she,* as common gender, just as a number of Far Eastern, Pacific, and East European languages express themselves to this day, since they do not employ the concept of gender.

4. We note with interest in the Genesis stories how this need of three to represent true family life is experienced. At Gen. 1:27 God creates the primal two, the male and the female. He does so that they might "be fruitful and multiply," i.e., begin the succession of families that was God's will and purpose for mankind. At Gen. 4:1 we read that the man "knew" his wife. The verb *yada'* here describes that total knowledge of one another, including the sex act, that results from perfect love. The actual result of their intercourse was that the woman conceived, and a baby was born. The mystery of childbirth strikes Eve forcibly. "I have gotten 'a male human being' *with* Yahweh," she exclaims. What was born of her body, she recognized, was not merely the result of a natural process. On the other hand, we must not say it was "supernatural," for no such idea exists in the Hebrew Scriptures. What we call natural and supernatural are one throughout the OT.

The particle *eth* can have two meanings. It can mark the object of a verb if the noun be definite. Here then Eve would be saying, "I have gotten a man, that is to say, Yahweh." On the other hand, *eth* can mean simply "with," in which case she says "I have gotten a man, with Yahweh," that is to say, "with the help of the LORD." Both translations are difficult. The first, which is perfectly possible grammatically, leads to an astonishing statement. The second is debatable in that there exists a word for "with," *'im,* about whose translation there is no doubt at all. So we ask why the sacred author chose to use a term that could give a doubtful meaning. What we should notice, however, is that never again in the OT does any mother ever make such an astounding statement as here. So we are led to the conclusion that this one instance is sufficient for the purposes of revelation. "Father" and "Mother" had already been created in the image and likeness of God. Now, however, they had entered into a new relationship, not only to God and to each other, but also to one whom they received, either "with" the Lord, or *as* the Lord himself. This third party could now be added to the two who were already created in the image of God, to make a triune revelation in human flesh. This results in a revelation of the nature of *elohim*, the usual word for "God" in the OT. As George M. Newlands declares in *Theology of the Love of God:* "The love of God has a trinitarian structure" (32).

5. The analogy of three human beings in mutual love and in communion together with *elohim* could possibly break down, however, when we learn (e.g., at Isa. 31:3) that God is Spirit and not flesh. But there are two things to say of Spirit here: (1) The Spirit is no ghost. The Spirit of God, for the prophets, means the power of God in loving action, and certainly not the idea of static Being. (2) OT people, on the analogy of their own experience of love, constantly envisioned God as being "clothed" with a "body."

It is not ridiculous to say such a thing, in that mankind—male and female together—is certainly composed of both body and spirit, and it is as such that *adam* is made in the image of God. In the same way, the OT thinkers never suggested that God was mere naked Spirit. God "wore" his glory as a man "wears" his body. In the NT we find this awareness carried forward. There the Church is called the body of Christ; so it is only through the Church that the world can learn that Christ is not naked Spirit either. We note also that, right at the beginning of his ministry, the Spirit descended upon Jesus at his baptism—how hesitantly the Gospels speak!—"like a dove." Only Luke adds the word "bodily."

6. Humanity can gaze in wonder and love at the glory of God, for it is something we can "see," whether by eye or by mind. In like manner, we read, God gazes at Zion in love, his Bride whom he plans to "marry" (Isa. 62:3-5). God's glory is the external manifestation of the divine essence, which is holiness.

Theological thinking, right up to the Reformation, was bedeviled by its heritage of Greek dualism. This view of reality would not allow the Person of God to be conceived as having anything to do with "flesh." In fact, even today groups within Christendom tend to feel shocked at any such suggestion. In doing so they reveal how near they are to the very old Christian heresy of Docetism. Human love cannot exist as an ethereal, spiritual sentiment. It requires the body as well as the spirit, not in order to *be* love, but in order to *exercise* love. In fact, the human being loves and hates even with his *kelayot*, his kidneys! (Jer. 11:20). This view the editor of Songs of course took for granted. He would agree with Jeremiah that the word for God's glory, *kabod*, might alternatively be vowelled as *kabed*, his liver! (Jer. 2:11; Exod. 33:22).

7. God is spoken of some eight times in the OT as a *nephesh*. This Hebrew word is the normal term for a human person's whole personality: body, soul, and spirit. The person's body, his *basar,* his flesh, is visible, but his spirit is not. Likewise God's glory is visible, in the form of his *"basar,"* his "back," but his "face" *(paneh),* the window into his essential Being, is not (Exod. 33:20). (For a full discussion of this issue, see my *From Moses to Paul: A Christological Study in the Light of Our Hebraic Heritage* [1949], ch. 2). We have no right to set such thinking aside, on the ground that it is merely an anthropomorphic way of speaking; for the greatest anthropomorphic "utterance" of all time was made when Jesus declared: "He who has seen me, has seen the Father."

The tradition of Israel was always to use personal language when God was mentioned. God, to Israel, was not just *a* person; he was the normative person. He was not an "It." In line with this OT conception therefore, Abraham Heschel could write: "Plato thinks of God in the image of an idea; the prophets think of God in the image of personal presence."

P. A. H. de Boer finds an analogy to the above in the Wisdom passage in Prov. 8:22-31 *(Fatherhood and Motherhood in Israelite and Judean Piety* [1974], 5). There Wisdom is known as the "daughter" of God, or as "the beloved little mother" (reading *ha-immon* for *haomen*); "her play . . . would be the loveplay from which the universe was born." De Boer quotes Erminie H. Lantero, *Feminine Aspects of Divinity* (13), as he speaks of "a fleeting suggestion of marital joys."

8. We have noted in the Commentary that HE is not HER "boss," her *ba'al* in the Canaanite sense, and SHE is not HIS slave. Each in turn sees his/her beloved in terms of the loveliness of the nature that God has created. Nature, however, is not complete and perfect in itself; it is racked with droughts, earthquakes, famines, and diseases. Our couple, however, have been created by God to live in the world as part of its as yet incomplete or perhaps, rather, unfulfilled nature. So they must necessarily learn both the agony and the ecstasy of the love that God has ordained for them to experience.

We see how they make a joyful discovery together. They discover that the total self-giving of two persons to each other is no less than "very heaven" (the term we used in the Commentary).

In line with the whole of OT revelation, our couple behave in insouciant awareness that each is not a temporary union of body and soul. We have emphasized that such was the basic philosophy of the Greeks; but so also was it that of the Egyptians, the Canaanites, and, later on, the Romans; in fact, to this day it is the view of that religion with which the Greeks came into contact in the days of the Hellenistic Empire, the Hindu religion of India. The OT person, on the other hand, never suggests that "mankind has a soul." He would wholly reject the Greek saying: *Soma sema*, "the body is a tomb." Rather, the OT person recognized that mankind's erotic instincts are one with their highest intellectual and spiritual pursuits, whereas the view that the body is a tomb is almost a dogma in most forms of the Eastern religions that the West is meeting in this generation. That, then, is why the physical act of the consummation of their union by our two unsophisticated *Israelite* young people, who are wholly and completely "in love," is a total experience that is at once both thrilling and utterly satisfying.

9. Self-love, again, such as we find described for us in the Greek myth of Narcissus, is quite other than the love we meet with in Holy Scripture. Narcissus was a beautiful young man who went in seach of love, but he found that to search for it brought no results. One day he chanced to see his own reflection in a pool of water, and promptly fell in love with it. Yet he gradually came to feel no satisfaction in such self-love, and slowly he withered away and died, unfulfilled.

If self-love is not true love, neither is the mutual love of two persons for each other. For such love can descend to the level of being merely "self-love multiplied by two."

What the order of the succession of the poems in Songs "reveals" to us is that it requires a minimum of *three* persons, each loving the other two—in other words, a happy family—for the meaning of true love to become available to human hearts. Not only so, but such true love is shown to be "eschatological," i.e., it is revealed as belonging to and coming from the other side of death.

In Hosea 3 we discover that this very human husband recognized that he was not purposing to take back home his adulterous wife because *he* thought that he ought to do so; rather, he found that it was *God* who was putting the thought and the plan to do so into his sinful mind. Thus, in obeying the thought, he found that it meant receiving a revelation of what God not only *would do* but actually already *had done* with his people Israel. If Hosea, then, knew that he had received a revelation of the love of God, so also our editor, in ruminating on the content of the poems he held in his hands, discovered—even as he placed them in order—that he was receiving a revelation both of the nature and of the plan of the living God.

10. The word "God" in Hebrew *(elohim)* is plural ("Let *us* make man in *our* image" [Gen. 1:26]), yet it is rendered in English by a

singular noun, "God." When the young Isaiah, as a sinner, experiences an overwhelming confrontation with the holiness of Yahweh (a singular noun), he hears the LORD say: "Whom shall I send, and who will go for *us*?" (Isa. 6:8), here using a plural. It would seem that the deity is both singular and plural at the same time, both "I" and "we."

In Ps. 8, where the deity is addressed as Yahweh, and where we meet with the words "How majestic is *thy* name . . ." (singular), the poem continues: "The son of man . . . thou hast made him little less than God (*elohim*, plural)." This word the LXX felt bound to translate by "angels," so shocked were its editors, it would seem, by its abruptness.

Some interpreters contend that such plural language is a relic of a pre-Mosaic theology, when God was pictured as a kind of chairman presiding over a council of heavenly beings. Probably God was indeed so regarded in very early days, in line with the pagan thought of the period, as shown in the Ugaritic literature we now possess. But once again, we are presented with the fallacy that a word must necessarily mean to its user what its root meant originally to other generations before.

Of course, such a conception could be held pictorially long after Israel was adamantly sure of its monotheistic apprehension of God. Thus, in the book of Daniel, the Almighty is described as "the ancient of days . . . his raiment was white as snow, and the hair of his head like pure wool" (Dan. 7:9). Here he is clearly the chairman of a court sitting in judgment, even though the good folk of the 2nd cent. B.C. would never have taken this description literally. This was because before the era of precise theological definition Israel was aware that a description of the nature of God was not exhausted when he was spoken of as "one" *(ehad)*.

The basic Semitic root *el* should not be equated with *elohim* to mean "God" in its OT sense. Rather, it should be translated by the idea of "divine being," a concept acceptable to peoples of all nations. For *el* is common to the religions of the ancient Near East as the supreme "god." We must be clear that *elohim* is the God of the Covenant; he is not the "god" of the nations. Consequently, he is to be equated with Yahweh, an equation found first in Gen. 2-3. Psalm 50:1 actually has *el elohim yahweh* (RSV "the Mighty One, God the LORD") as the name of Israel's God.

Of course, the name *eloah,* a singular noun, also occurs for God, but it came to be discarded for the theologically rich term *elohim*. Outside the book of Job *eloah* occurs only a handful of times (e.g.,

Isa. 44:8; Hab. 3:3; Ps. 50:22; 139:19). Each time, moreover, it reads like a deliberate archaism; e.g., Isa. 44:8 refers to the ancient song of Moses (Deut. 32), and at Hab. 3:3 it refers to an ancient theophany. The psalms like to teach their readers to remember that their faith comes down the arches of the years. The name's 42 occurrences in Job, however, poses another question. We can only speculate that, since its background is that of the geographical area that is now Arabia, this title for God spoke more significantly in a region that later became the home ground of many Christian heresies and that opted to name the divine being by the singular term *Allah.*

Deut. 6:4 has given Israel its basic creed, as used to this day by every Jew: "Hear, O Israel: Yahweh our God is one, Yahweh." This sentence is expressible in still three further ways, as shown in the margin of the RSV. The Hebrew word used here, *ehad* ("one") occurs some 650 times in the OT, usually representing the mathematical symbol for "one." But it can also represent the idea of uniqueness (1 Kgs. 4:19; Ezek. 7:5), though "unique" is normally expressed by another word from the same root, *yahid,* thus: "Take your son, your only son . . . Isaac, whom you love" (Gen. 22:2, 16). The LXX actually translates this instance of "only" by *agapetos,* "beloved," as it does again at Prov. 4:3; Jer. 6:26; Amos 8:10; Zech. 12:10 (cf. Matt. 3:17). This connection between "unique" and "beloved" is exemplified at Ps. 22:20, where *yahid* is paralleled with *naphshi,* "my life," meaning "my unique possession."

How then are we to understand *ehad*? Actually, it can convey two meanings at once, both the mathematical symbol and the idea of comprehensiveness. Thus Isa. 51:2 can speak of Abraham and Sarah as being Israel's *one* ancestor. Or again, at Ezek. 37:17a, the word of the Lord bids the prophet take two sticks, and join them together into one stick (*ehadim,* plural!).

Most important to this end is the basic description of the nature of mankind at Gen. 2:24. A man "cleaves to his wife, and they become one *(ehad)* flesh," yet of course they remain two persons. This adjective can thus be used to mean both "unique" and "one whole" at the same time. As such it is used even of Yahweh: "On that day Yahweh shall be *ehad* and his name *ehad*" (Zech. 14:9). Moreover, the rabbinical scholars who preserved the text of the OT and passed it on to us with meticulous care, regarded the word *elohim* in the same light. Visible only to the student of Hebrew, the "sacred tetragrammaton" (i.e., the Hebrew consonants *yhwh,* "Yahweh") is not normally written as such. Almost universally throughout the OT the divine name is written as *adonai,* meaning "my lords," in the plural.

53

All writers are careful to use the singular *adoni* when addressing a human master. Would they have done so if they had not "felt" the comprehensiveness of the Godhead as well as its uniqueness? (For a fuller discussion of this issue, see my "The LORD is one," *ET* 79 [1967]: 8-10.)

Adon was a general Semitic word meaning "lord." It occurs in Adonis, the name of one of the Syrian gods, who presided over the crucial realm of agriculture. Ancient Greece formed a magical cult of Adonis worship. But the OT is determined to show that Israel's *adon* is not Adonis, but *adonai* (plural, like the word *elohim*).

Finally in this regard, we suggest that the apostle Paul had to search for a way to express this comprehensiveness of *elohim* when he was compelled to use the singular term *theos* for God when writing in Greek for a world audience. To have used the plural of *theos* would have necessarily conveyed to the Hellenistic world the view that the Jews and Christians alike were polytheists. So he interprets the oneness *(ehad)* of God that is the basic creed of Scripture by speaking of God's *pleroma,* his "fulness" (Eph. 3:19; Col. 1:19). He did so on the basis of such a passage as Jer. 23:24: "Do I not fill heaven and earth?" Nowhere, of course, in the OT does the word "trinity" occur. Consequently, Karl Barth must write: "God is less trinity than triune" (*Church Dogmatics* 1/1 §8:1).

12. God is thus the "wholeness of the plurality," not so much of a "family" in heaven as of the "sacramental union of personality." We see such a concept in Jewish and Christian marriage, or as it is represented in the covenantal relationship between God and Israel that God gave to his people at Sinai. Since the Godhead in the OT is nowhere described as a family, the use of "Father" for God is to be seen in context. For throughout the OT, when God is spoken of as Father, the meaning is always that of "Progenitor of the race." And as for Mother, the wholeness of God has indeed many motherly aspects to it, but certainly we do not find in the OT that God's "wholeness" could be addressed as Mother. (For the fulness of God, see Eduard Schweizer, *The Letter to the Colossians* [Minneapolis: Augsburg, 1982], 76-79.)

The comprehensiveness as well as the uniqueness of God that the editor of Songs "felt in his bones," even as did the rabbis and later on the Masoretes (who preserved the text of the OT), made him think as a theologian and not as a logician or a philosopher. The description of the requirements of true love, as put there by God, that can be seen in the relationship of a sincere human couple (who are also concerned together for "little sister") is therefore revelation of the love that must obtain within the Godhead, in whose image God himself created the couple. As Jürgen Moltmann says in *The Trinity and the Kingdom* (57): "If God is love he is at once the lover, the beloved and the love itself."

Troy Organ, writing in *The Christian Century,* quotes that statement by Moltmann, and then adds: "God is Beloved-Lover-Love" ("Oxymorons as Theological Symbols," 28 November 1984, 1130). He claims also that the Holy Spirit is the feminine principle of the Godhead, claiming that God is actually Father-Mother-Son.

13. Karl Rahner declares that "trinitarian theology is meant above all to be a truth about salvation." In Songs HE saves HER from her natural self-centeredness, and SHE saves HIM likewise. SHE sees forgiveness as "casting his sins behind her back"; HE, with total sincerity can declare: "My girl is an angel"—even when outsiders see that she is not. HE never mentions HER sins or imperfections, nor SHE his. Their sins are as if they were not, for in their "place" they now see only grace. And if this is too difficult an idea for us to grasp, we might translate the content of the word "grace" into that other word that derives from it, "graciousness." By so doing, we learn to see grace as an event, as an act of a living person expressed through the flesh as something you can "see."

On the other hand, as Rahner points out, their love for each other is not automatic. In parallel with this, then, God can and does withdraw from our experience of him (Songs 3:1; 6:1). That is why the psalmist's cry can arise as a human experience in relation to God: "Why hast thou forsaken me?" (Ps. 22:1).

Philosophically speaking, love is considered to be a "sentiment." Not so in the OT. The latter shows us a personal, active God who is always pictured for us dramatically *in action,* acting as a human person acts. But since "human person" covers both sexes, the nature of the Godhead as *love* must be (1) as a male acts, (2) as a female acts, and (3) as a child acts, all within the *one* fellowship. For example, just as Adam delighted in Eve, so God delighted—*with his sons*—in his creative activity (Job 38:7). Even the divine name Yahweh does not indicate God's eternal being; rather, it reveals his action and presence in historical affairs (Exod. 3:14 RSV mg.).

14. We noted that our young couple had to experience the agony of love as well as its ecstasy. In *The Prophets* ([1962], 483), the Jewish scholar Abraham Joshua Heschel, with reference to Ps. 139:7-18, maintains that it is not possible to speak of Yahweh's *pathos* unless such is a plural experience. Heschel notes that for the Greeks "existence is experiencing being," whereas in the OT "exis-

tence is experiencing concern." This means that through revelation one can learn "to sense God's participation in existence," or actually to "experience oneself as a divine secret." Hosea, the prophet who speaks loudest about the love of God, can declare, God speaking, "My heart recoils within me" (Hos. 11:8 RSV). This phrase is literally "my insides are turned upside down," "my compassion grows warm and tender" or "grows hot," "agitated," "burnt up."

In the Second Commandment (Exod. 20:5) we have the words: "I Yahweh your God am *el qannah*," a God who feels his creative love for Israel as "gnawing at his bones" (Prov. 14:30). Gottfried Quell (*TDNT* 3 [1965]: 1078) even suggests that the word which we translate by "jealous" reveals God as a young God who is very much like the young lover in Songs! In a word, God's creative purpose both for the birth of the New Israel and for the bringing to birth of the New Creation comes about through the pain which belongs at the heart of love.

But this self-giving defies the pain. In our poems each gives to the other, not looking to receive. Giving implies action. Thus we are shown that love is not a static essence but a movement, growth, development, and all in the realm that includes the flesh. Songs, in fact, is that strange type of literature among the religions of the contemporary ancient world which is an affirmation of the flesh.

We may illustrate this "corporate creative activity" on the part of the young couple by means of the pictorial theology that is basic to the OT way of revelation. Just as Adam needs Eve to complete and realize the love that God intends mankind to know, so God needs his people Israel to exemplify totally the reality of the love of the Godhead. He makes covenant with Israel (Exod. 19:5-6) in love and with a loving purpose.

According to the prophets, God's saving act of love is known as his *tsedeq*. Isaiah, followed by Deutero-Isaiah and then Trito-Isaiah, employs the feminine form of this root *(tsedaqah)* to describe that which God places in the heart of mankind once mankind has received God's *tsedeq*. This feminine term describes what mankind does, or should do, in response to God's original act of love. Too often it is translated merely by "righteousness." Unfortunately in today's world that word, and the expression "the righteous," used to describe the covenant people, have become the opposite of what the Hebrew word intends. For today a "righteous" person is regarded by many as that objectionable being, a "self-righteous" person. Rather, we should allow the feminine term to echo the masculine that is used of God's action, and thus render it by "creative" or "saving love." (See the argument in *Servant Theology,* esp. 92, in the *International Theological Commentary*.) For Songs has nothing to say about morals, only about love (cf. 1 Cor. 13); and it recognizes love as God's gift to humanity, to do with even as he does with us. It is "not of this world," it comes "out of eternity."

16. Step by step the prophets of Israel come to discover that the love of God can best be understood in terms of marriage. This realization arose from God's action in "making covenant" with Israel, as we read of this at Exod. 19. The prophets make the otherwise fantastic affirmation that the living God is the Bridegroom and Israel is the Bride (e.g., Hos. 1–3), unworthy as she may be of the honor (Jer. 2:23-25; Ezek. 16:37-39). The prophets dared to take the metaphor of marriage from the cult of Baal, and boldly called the Lord "husband." But, as Hos. 1–3 makes clear, they totally separated "love" as the worship of the Baals (a plural term) from that of love for *elohim* (also a plural term), and could apply it directly to love of Yahweh. This we saw earlier in our argument.

Since in ancient Israel there was evidently a ceremony of betrothal, of "getting engaged," which was regarded as being as definitive as marriage itself, the prophets represent Yahweh as speaking of his jealous love for Israel his Bride (cf. Exod. 20:5) when she was really only his "fiancée." He declares that no other people, no "female" can ever steal away his love for Israel, and, in reverse that he will permit no other god, "male," to cuckold him in his relationship with his female Beloved. Moreover, when Israel was in exile, when she supposed that God had divorced her (Isa. 54:4-8), God had to demand that she show him the certificate of divorce that an Israelite husband must write out if he sends away his wife (Deut. 24:1-4; Isa. 50:1). Instead of that, God repeats to his Beloved: "I, I am he that comforts you" (Isa. 51:12), Thus, once the long period of the exile, of "separation from God" is over, God promises to the remnant that had returned to rebuild both Jerusalem and their faith, through the lips of Trito-Isaiah (Isa. 62:4-5): "You shall no more be termed Forsaken, . . . but you shall be called My delight is in her . . . and as the bridegroom rejoices over the bride, so shall your God rejoice over you"—exactly what HE does over HER in Songs. This statement is a promise, then, that the day shall indeed come when God shall "consummate" his marriage with Israel.

Luke 2:25 tells us that there was a righteous (see above for the meaning of this adjective) and devout man in Jerusalem named Simeon, who was "looking for the consolation *(paraklesis)* of Israel" (the word employed in the LXX at Isa. 51:12, quoted above). That then would be the moment when God would take his Bride and "console" her in love, again just as HE did with HER in Songs. By doing so, God would become "one flesh" with Israel his Bride, and would then be "married" to her. Of that union there would now be born a baby, not this time "with Yahweh" but "with the Holy Spirit." This baby would then be one flesh of both God and of mankind, and so would be at once both son of God and son of man. Moreover, he would be conceived in his mother's vineyard: "Let me sing for my beloved a love song concerning his vineyard" (Isa. 5:1). This was a name given to Israel by prophets and psalmists alike.

17. From this we can also discover that what applies to Israel, the people of God, when God's love in covenant "comforts" his covenant people can also apply to us as individuals who are also members of the covenant people. As Karl Barth puts it, it is through this revealed order that an individual may find a personal faith (*Church Dogmatics* 4/1-3). Moreover, he adds that once one has discovered himself to be a child of the Covenant he need not seek farther for a meaning to his life. For life's meaning is embedded in love.

18. These three points are thus in order. (1) God does not reject the plain realities of the physical bodies of his creatures. As the *Te Deum Laudamus* puts it: "Thou didst not abhor the Virgin's womb." (2) When the word became flesh it identified itself with the flesh of the human body. The body's various parts may, of course, be used with greedy, sexual aims in view; thus Paul could say: "For our sake he made him to be sin who knew no sin" (2 Cor. 5:21). (3) Since love is creative, and just as God used the chaos that was in the beginning to create light, so also in the same way he used the human body, with all its potentialities for sin, to initiate the dawn of the kingdom of God.

19. Herein then we see the uniqueness of the biblical view of love. Mahayana Buddhism, for example, seeks for its devotees nonattachment to the realm of things, including the human body. When they attain this nonattachment, the enlightened are concurrently filled with compassion toward all; yet they experience compassion only as a vague sentiment, never specific. It is like the vague claim of certain so-called Christians when they exclaim "I love all babies."

Songs, then, becomes for us no less than revelation. It reveals several realities in this respect. (1) Divine love is not what the world understands by love. (2) There is no such thing as love in itself, but only persons loving persons. (3) Love cannot be "there" in the heavens as something in itself, any more than on earth. (4) Present-day enlightened Hinduism is wrong when it declares that "love is God." No, says Songs, "God is love." (5) When SHE said: "*We* have a little sister, and *we* are concerned for her in love," she was echoing what God had declared time without number to his Bride. "*We* have a little sister—namely the poor, the desolate, the outcasts of the gentile world—specifically for whose salvation 'our' Covenant was created."

20. An important point to note is that in the whole series of poems no reference is ever made to questions of morality. No reference is ever made to the Ten Commandments. Western culture is obstinately blind to its Judaeo-Christian heritage. It seeks to counteract the "chaos" of modern Western culture by teaching children "ethics" at school. But, as the great Greek philosophers have shown us, ethical living may be different in Athens from what it was in Sparta, different in France now from what it is in China, different in the present day from what it was in the Victorian era. Teaching morals (or ethics) cannot stem the waves of chaos. What Songs shows us is that true love, the love that is the gift of the God of the Covenant, wholly alters the bent of human nature. The morality that is evidenced to us by divine revelation altogether depends upon the transformation of the nature of the human personality. Thereupon mankind's moral choices flow naturally from the heart as the fruits of love; men and women will not have to become philosophers or theosophists to discover what they ought to do in any given situation. Not only so, but they can maintain this vision of the meaning of life all their days so long as they "abide" in the love of God. Songs itself does not theologize. It merely proclaims reality.

21. In a sense, Songs brings the work of the great prophets to a conclusion. These great individuals expressed the Word of Yahweh in a form that unsophisticated humanity could "see," since they uttered the thoughts, emotions, and intentions of the living God through the framework of human thinking. The result was, as Dale Patrick puts it, that "the audience is forced to enter into Yahweh's inner life" (*The Rendering of God in the Old Testament* [1981], 24). Songs now reveals that these are the natural outflow from the fact that the nature of God is love. Moreover, since knowledge of God does not happen to us in a flash, love—as a "growing together," as Songs shows—becomes the joyous adventure of life. It had been offered to God's people from the days of Moses: "I will *become* with you" (Exod. 3:12), as God had declared to that patriarch through the medium of a language that has no verb "to be" (Hebrew can express the idea of "being" only through the noun *yesh*, meaning "exis-

tence"). In Songs we are able to "see" the ultimate behind all religions, no matter what their adherents "believe." This is because every human being knows what it means to fall in love.

22. Again, Songs reveals to us that Israel is the one and only people through whom God could have opened the eyes of mankind to discover what he is like and what he is performing in history. It was Israel alone among the nations that knew nothing of a separation between matter and spirit, body and soul, as we have stressed more than once. Love envelopes the whole of the human *nephesh*. Consequently, it was in Israel alone that the Incarnation could have taken place. Only in her could the word have become flesh and dwelt among us. So too with the converse: only in Israel could the flesh, as part of the total *nephesh* of Jesus, have been taken up into God at the Resurrection.

23. In biblical thought, however, there is one decisive division, one great separating factor. It is not that of the Greeks or of the religions of the East. It is the division between Good and Evil, symbolized by God when he "separated" them at Creation, under the figures of day and night, light and darkness (Gen. 1:3-5). In Christ, however, we meet with one who was light itself and was thus without sin (Heb. 4:15; in fact, the whole Letter to the Hebrews deals with this issue), so that in him the very idea of "separation" is a nonissue.

24. In this way, then, Songs "materialized myth." Knowledge of God, the incomparable, "whose thoughts are not our thoughts" and "whose ways are past finding out," is beyond all human philosophies and dreams. In days gone by, Jews regarded Songs as a "myth" of the ways of God with Israel, and Christians as a "myth" showing Christ's love for his Church. If these had been the final interpretations of the book, then in today's world we would have been bereft of a revelation that meets our needs. But we are to see these two "myths" as analogies of what Songs really declares. It begins with fact, the fact of human love, and continues to show that true and jealous love, along with the total commitment of two persons to each other in utter self-denial, is not something that could have ever formed a mere link in the chain of human evolution, but something that can be understood only as a gift from God. The fact of its being a gift removes Songs from the whole area of myth and of human religious values, and renders the book a vehicle of revelation. Moreover, in actuality, all human beings, of whatever religion, race, or culture, if they experience true and total self-giving love the one for the other, know in their hearts that they are in touch with the

divine. For they can perceive in themselves the power of God's love, and can discover that love transforms naturally selfish and self-centered persons into creatively concerned and compassionate human beings. This new integrity of personality that they discover in each other they then recognize can be nothing else than a gift from God, and so be a revelation of the very nature of the God who gives it.

BIBLIOGRAPHY

Books

Carr, G. Lloyd. *The Song of Solomon.* Tyndale Old Testament Commentaries (Leicester and Downers Grove: Inter-Varsity, 1984).

Delitzsch, Franz. *Proverbs, The Song of Songs and Ecclesiastes.* Commentary on the Old Testament, ed. C. F. Keil and Delitzsch (1872; repr. Grand Rapids: Wm. B. Eerdmans, 1984).

Dryburgh, Bob. *Lessons from Lovers in the Song of Solomon* (New Canaan, CT: Keats, 1975).

Falk, Marcia. *Love Lyrics from the Bible* (Sheffield: Almond, 1982).

Feuillet, André. *Le Cantique des Cantiques.* Lectio Divina (Paris: Éditions du Cerf, 1953).

Gordis, Robert. *The Songs of Songs* (New York: Jewish Theological Seminary of America, 1954).

Harper, Andrew. *The Song of Solomon.* Cambridge Bible for Schools and Colleges (Cambridge: Cambridge University Press, 1907).

Ibn Ezra, Abraham ben Meir. *Commentary on the Canticles,* ed. H. J. Matthews (London: Trübner, 1874).

Jay, Peter. *The Song of Songs* (London: Anvil Press Poetry, 1975).

Landy, Francis. *Paradoxes of Paradise: Identity and Difference in the Song of Songs* (Sheffield: Almond, 1983).

Origen. *The Song of Songs: Commentary and Homilies,* ed. R. P. Lawson. Ancient Christian Writers (Westminster, MD: 1957).

Pope, Marvin H. *Song of Songs.* Anchor Bible (Garden City: Doubleday, 1977).

Rudolph, Wilhelm. *Das Buch Ruth. Das Hohelied. Die Klagelieder.* Kommentar zum Alten Testament (Gütersloh: Gerd Mohn, 1962).

Schneekloth, I. G. *The Targum of the Song of Songs* (dissertation, Madison: University of Wisconsin, 1977).

Scott, David Russell. *Pessimism and Love in Ecclesiastes and the Song of Songs* (London: James Clarke, 1915).

White, John Bradley. *A Study of the Language of Love in the Song of Songs and Ancient Egyptian Poetry.* Society of Biblical Literature Dissertation (Missoula: Scholars Press, 1978).

Articles

Cohen, Gerson D. "The Song of Songs and the Jewish Religious Mentality," in *The Canon and Masorah of the Hebrew Bible*, ed. S. Z. Leiman (New York: Ktav, 1974), 262-282.

Dubarle, André M. "L'Amour humain dans le Cantique des Cantiques," *Revue Biblique* 61 (1954):67-86.

Driver, Godfrey Rolles. "Supposed Arabisms in the Old Testament," *Journal of Biblical Literature* 55 (1936): 101-120.

Honeyman, Alexander Mackie. "Two Contributions to Canaanite Topography," *Journal of Theological Studies* 50 (1949): 50-52.

Knight, George A. F. "The LORD is one," *Expository Times* 79 (1967): 8-10.

Organ, Troy. "Oxymorons as Theological Symbols," *Christian Century*, 28 November 1984, 1128-1130.

Quell, Gottfried. "Κυριος," *Theological Dictionary of the New Testament* 3, ed. Gerhard Kittel (Grand Rapids: Wm. B. Eerdmans, 1965): 1058-1081.

Rowley, H. H. "The Interpretation of the Song of Songs," in *The Servant of the Lord and Other Essays on the Old Testament*, 2nd ed. (Oxford: Blackwell, 1965), 195-245.

Sadgrove, M. "The Song of Songs as Wisdom Literature," *Studia Biblica* 1, ed. E. A. Livingstone. Sixth International Congress on Biblical Studies (Sheffield: JSOT, 1978), 245-248.

Segal, Moses H. "The Song of Songs," *Vetus Testamentum* 12 (1962): 470-490.

Würthwein, Ernst. "Zum Verständnis des Hohenliedes," *Theologische Rundschau* 32 (1967): 177-212.

Other Works

deBoer, P. A. H. *Fatherhood and Motherhood in Israelite and Judean Piety* (Leiden: Brill, 1974).

Driver, Godfrey Rolles. *Canaanite Myths and Legends*. Old Testament Studies (Edinburgh: T. & T. Clark, 1956).

Dulles, Avery R. *Models of Revelation* (Garden City: Doubleday, 1983).

Heschel, Abraham Joshua. *The Prophets* (New York: Harper & Row, 1962).

Knight, George A. F. *From Moses to Paul: A Christological Study in the Light of Our Hebraic Heritage* (London: Lutterworth, 1949).

——. *The New Israel*. International Theological Commentary (Grand Rapids: Wm. B. Eerdmans and Edinburgh: Handsel, 1985).

——. *Ruth and Jonah*. Torch Bible Commentaries (London: SCM, 1950).

Lantero, Erminie H. *Feminine Aspects of Divinity* (Wallingford, PA: Pendle Hill, 1973).

Lys, Daniel. *Le plus beau chant de la création* (Paris: Éditions du Cerf, 1968).

Moltmann, Jürgen. *The Trinity and the Kingdom: The Doctrine of God* (San Francisco: Harper & Row and London: SCM, 1981).

Newlands, George M. *Theology of the Love of God* (London: Collins, 1980, and Atlanta: John Knox, 1981).

Patrick, Dale. *The Rendering of God in the Old Testament.* Overtures to Biblical Theology (Philadelphia: Fortress, 1981).

Schweizer, Eduard. *The Letter to the Colossians* (Minneapolis: Augsburg and London: SPCK, 1982).

Széles, Maria Eszenyei. *Wrath and Mercy.* International Theological Commmentary (Grand Rapids: Wm. B. Eerdmans and Edinburgh: Handsel, 1987).

Trible, Phyllis. *God and the Rhetoric of Sexuality.* Overtures to Biblical Theology (Philadelphia: Fortress, 1978).

Zimmerli, Walther. *I Am Yahweh* (Atlanta: John Knox, 1982).

DIVINE REPENTANCE

A Commentary on the Book of
Jonah

FRIEDEMANN W. GOLKA

To My Mother

CONTENTS

Author's Preface   68

Introduction   70

1:1-3   Jonah's Call and Disobedience   73

1:4-6   God's Response and the Sailors' Peril   78

1:7-10   The Culprit Identified   81

1:11-16   The Solution and Its Unexpected Consequences   85

1:17–2:10   A Strange Prayer from the Belly of the Fish   89
         Digression I: The Authorship of the Jonah "Psalm"   90

3:1-3   The Second Call and Jonah's Obedience   101

3:4-5   Instant Success in Nineveh   104

3:6-9   The Royal Response   108

3:10   The Divine Repentance   112

4:1-4   Jonah's Outburst   114
         Digression II: Ra'ah—Evil, Calamity, Divine
         Punishment, Wickedness   114

4:5-11   An Ironic Instruction in Divine Pity   121

The Message of the Book of Jonah   125

Epilogue: The Sign of Jonah   129

Bibliography   133

AUTHOR'S PREFACE

The book of Jonah and its interpretation reflect the common history of Jews and Christians. The argument about Jonah is at the same time the argument of two world religions about a common heritage. It is here that the strongest Christian anti-Judaism appears; it is here that the Jewish exegesis always finds itself on the defensive. But it is here, too—after Auschwitz!—that Jewish and Christian interpretations seem to converge more than anywhere else.

Jonah is, therefore, a crucial text for the Jewish-Christian dialogue. For this reason my first thanks must go to my Jewish friends, Rabbis Dr. Jonathan Magonet of Leo Baeck College, London, and Dan Cohn-Sherbok of the University of Kent at Canterbury. The former through his own work helped me to understand the narrative art of the book of Jonah, while the latter has sharpened my mind for the problems of the Jewish-Christian dialogue.

The influence of my Heidelberg teachers, Professors Claus Westermann, Hans Walter Wolff, and Rolf Rendtorff, is everywhere present in this commentary. While they cannot be blamed for my conclusions, they have certainly kindled my love for the OT. My Heidelberg friends, Drs. Jürgen Kegler and Erhard Blum, have generously given of their time (and coffee!) to help me sort out my own ideas in conversation with them.

Thanks are due also to the University of Exeter for granting me study leave during the Trinity Term 1985 to complete this commentary, and in the Department of Theology in particular to my colleague, Dr. Alastair Logan, for his careful scrutiny of my typescript and to Mrs. Lyn Fisher and Mrs. Carolyn Wright, who in the chaos of the beginning of an academic year have typed the final version for publication.

Last, and most important, my thanks go to the editor of this series, Emeritus Professor G. A. F. Knight, whom I have never met, but who through his fatherly letters from the other side of the globe provided the encouragement that I needed to see this task through.

I have included two digressions of a more scholarly nature. Readers who find them too difficult should simply turn over these pages.

University of Exeter,
Devon, U.K.
October 1985
FRIEDEMANN W. GOLKA

INTRODUCTION:
TIME AND BACKGROUND

Of the twelve Minor Prophets, the book of Jonah is the odd one out. It is not a collection of prophetic oracles like the other eleven, but a story. It is a didactic narrative, to be precise, with strong satirical overtones. So, who is its author and whom and what does he want to teach?

The book's name is derived from the 8th cent. prophet Jonah ben Amittai from Gath-hepher in Galilee. He was active as a prophet of salvation at the time of Jeroboam II (787-747 B.C.). 2 Kings 14:25-26 mentions that Jonah ben Amittai announced Jeroboam's restoration of the old border of Israel in spite of the latter's persistence in "the sins of Jeroboam [I] the son of Nebat, which he made Israel to sin" (2 Kgs. 14:24). However, because of the many aramaisms used, there can be no question of a date for the book earlier than the Persian period. So, Jonah ben Amittai, who gave his name to the book, is not its author.

If the 6th cent. is the earliest possible date for the book of Jonah, the 3rd cent. would be the latest. As Sir. 49:10 refers to Jonah as part of the twelve Minor Prophets, the book cannot have originated any later than the end of the 3rd cent. However, as there are no signs of Hellenistic influence in Jonah, a date before 330 (Alexander's conquest of Palestine) remains preferable.

We are therefore concerned with the question of where exactly in the Persian period (6th-4th cents.) we wish to locate the author of the book of Jonah. As our exegesis will show in detail, there are close connections between Jonah and the book of Joel. Both prophets announce the possibility of divine repentance after human penance—Joel for Israel only, Jonah even for the Gentiles. As Jonah goes further than Joel—and Joel does not appear to be a "reactionary"—a date for Jonah soon after Joel might commend itself. As the date of the book of Joel is around 400 (cf. Rudolf Smend, *Die Entstehung des Alten Testaments,* 172), a date for Jonah *during the last hundred years of the Persian period* (430-330) cannot be far out. There are no historical allusions that allow us to be any more precise than this.

Not much is known about those hundred years between the missions of Ezra and Nehemiah and the appearance of Alexander the Great in Palestine. Scholars have attempted to shed some light on the conflicts of this period by postulating *parties* in postexilic Israel. Otto Plöger (*Theocracy and Eschatology*), and Paul D. Hanson (*The Dawn of Apocalyptic*) divide between utopians and visionaries on the one hand, and hierocrats, realists, and pragmatists on the other. Is salvation to be achieved through the cult of the Second Temple, or is Israel to wait for the dawn of a new aeon? These would have been the issues between the parties, according to these two scholars.

Morton Smith (*Palestinian Parties and Politics that Shaped the Old Testament*) regards separatists (exclusiveness) and assimilationists (universalism) as the two main religious parties. While it would be tempting for an expositor of the book of Jonah to jump on this particular bandwagon, Smith's methodology requires caution. He attributes to the OT literature of the time a majority viewpoint ("the winner writes the history books"). This leads Smith to make too generous assumptions about the suppressed minority view. It is better to admit our ignorance than to indulge in ill-founded speculation.

O. H. Steck ("Das Problem theologischer Strömungen in nachexilischer Zeit," *EvTh* 28 [1968]: 445-458) differentiates between the Chronicler (including Ezra and Nehemiah) and the penitential prayers of Ezra 9 and Neh. 1, 9, which reflect a viewpoint diametrically opposed to that of the Chronicler.

The Chronicler, according to Steck (p. 451), regards postexilic Israel as being in a state of salvation because the edict of Cyrus has led to the rebuilding of the temple and of the city of Jerusalem, and to the consolidation of the cultic congregation. The period of punishment for Israel's sins is over (cf. 2 Chr. 36:15-21), as Yahweh has "stirred up" the spirit of Cyrus (Ezra 1:1). Israel is separated from the guilt of preexilic generations, and the country has been recompensed for its lost sabbaths. For any new sins the cult provides atonement and forgiveness.

A totally different view of the postexilic situation can be found in the penitential prayers of Ezra 9 and Neh. 1, 9. The return of the exiles and the restoration of the Jewish community are but a small sign of God's mercy towards a people whose history of disobedience continues beyond the catastrophes of 722 and 587 into postexilic times (Steck, p. 453). According to the concept of these penitential prayers, the theological status of postexilic Israel is of a preliminary nature and still under God's judgment. One therefore still expects the future arrival of salvation, which will reunite all of Israel in their country and bring Yahweh's curse on their enemies who are still oppressing them (Steck, p. 455). This view of history, as opposed to that of the Chronicler, seemed fully justified in the Seleucid era when, under Antiochus IV Epiphanes, oppression from outside and inner apostasy showed that the time of salvation had not yet arrived (Steck, p. 455).

This assessment of the postexilic situation in the penitential prayers is close to the Deuteronomistic movement that wrote or rewrote Israel's history from the entry into Canaan until the release of Jehoiachin from his Babylonian prison in the spirit of the book of Deuteronomy. Both the Deuteronomistic movement and the "post-Deuteronomistic orthodoxy" (Rendtorff) reflected in the work of the Chronicler represent not just theological streams, but also social groupings—even if they are still difficult to identify. Jonah certainly does not fit these mainstreams. While the book shares in the Deuteronomistic theology of divine repentance brought about by human penitence, its universalism does not fit the picture painted by Steck.

However, our claim that the author of Jonah is an individualist rather than the exponent of a party view, does not seem to be so unlikely, since the same is probably true of the books of Job and Ecclesiastes, near contemporaries of Jonah. The protests of Job and Ecclesiastes against the assumption of an act-consequence relationship represent the voice of individuals that does not seem to have affected the broad Wisdom tradition, which reasserts itself with Sirach (Ecclesiasticus) and the Wisdom of Solomon.

The author of Jonah is not a person who writes a powerful manifesto on behalf of one group against another. He is, rather, a critical observer of his Jewish co-religionists, who has to use the form of a didactic narrative and the devices of irony and satire to put his point across. By doing so he has created a masterpiece of Hebrew narrative art.

JONAH'S CALL AND DISOBEDIENCE

1:1-3

---

1 "Now (Hebrew "and") the word of the LORD came (Hebrew "was") to Jonah." This sounds as if we are dealing with the *continuation* of a story. Something might have stood before this "and." Karl Budde ("Vermutungen zum 'Midrasch des Buches der Könige,'" *ZAW* 12 [1892]: 37-51) suggested that Jonah 1:1 might be the continuation of 2 Kgs. 14:25, continuing 2 Kings in the form of a *midrash*. Midrashim are commentaries and meditations on a biblical text that continue an idea expressed in the biblical passage.

We know of the existence of such a midrash on the book of Kings, because it is mentioned in 2 Chr. 24:27. However, as the book of Ruth also begins with "And it came to pass," it would appear that the form of the Hebrew *imperfect consecutive* had already become so fossilized that its use at the beginning of a biblical book would no longer suggest that something else must have gone before. The book of Jonah is therefore no midrash on 2 Kgs. 14:25, but an independent *didactic narrative*.

The word of the Lord *came* to Jonah as it came to Abraham in Gen. 15:1, 4 and to the kings and prophets throughout the ages. What we have before us is the process of *revelation*; Jonah receives a command. Revelation indicates a distance between God and humanity that it is trying to bridge. How different the situation is in Gen. 2-3: After the man's disobedience God simply walks in the garden and questions him (Gen. 3:8ff). God and humanity are still in the same time and space (the same goes for Gen. 4:1-16; 6:1-4; 6:5–9:19). However, all this changes after the great Flood. In the story of the Tower of Babel (Gen. 11:1-9) God already has to come "down to see the city and the tower, which the sons of men had built" (Gen. 11:5). He is no longer in the same space. In the Patriarchal History God appears (Gen. 12:7) and speaks (12:1) to Abraham. But some, possibly later, passages avoid such a direct address: in Gen. 20:3 God only comes to Abimelech in a dream. Jonah 1:1 uses matter-of-fact language, discouraging all speculations as to when, where, and how exactly Yahweh would have spoken to the prophet.

Equally scanty is our information about Jonah. All we learn is his father's name: Amittai. We can extract a little more information from 2 Kgs. 14:25, which says of King Jeroboam II of the northern kingdom: "He restored the border of Israel from the entrance of Hamath as far as the Sea of the Arabah, according to the word of the LORD, the God of Israel, which he spoke by his servant Jonah the son of Amittai, the prophet, who was from Gath-hepher." This Jonah ben Amittai is an 8th cent. B.C. prophet from the Galilaean town of Gath-hepher. His prophecy shows him to be a prophet of salvation for Israel and, by implication, one of judgment for the nations.

This 8th cent. Jonah ben Amittai our narrator chooses as the hero of his didactic story. As the language of the book of Jonah is clearly postexilic, the tale about this prophet has a ring of "once upon a time" about it.

Just compare the scantiness of this information with what Amos 1:1 tells us about Jonah ben Amittai's near contemporary: "The words of Amos, who was among the shepherds of Tekoa, which he saw concerning Israel in the days of Uzziah king of Judah and in the days of Jeroboam the son of Joash, king of Israel, two years before the earthquake." We learn the profession of Amos and a date. From the biblical chronology as well as the archaeological evidence concerning the earthquake, scholars can date Amos' ministry with some confidence around the year 760. Not so in Jonah 1:1, where what we have is just the name, Jonah ben Amittai. History is obviously not what matters in this story.

2   "Arise, go." The divine command to Jonah reminds us of the first biblical command of this nature. Israel's salvation history begins with the command to Abraham "Go from your country . . . to the land that I will show you" (Gen. 12:1). Jonah's journey is to be a reversal of Abraham's. Jonah is to leave Palestine heading northeast for Nineveh.

He is to go to Nineveh, the *great city*. Nineveh is mentioned nine times, and four of those times the narrator applies to it the epithet "that great city" (Jonah 1:2//3:2; 3:3; 4:11)—"great" being the favorite word of our author (fourteen times in the book).

Nineveh is clearly a legendary city for our author, who wrote a long time after its destruction in 612. He probably thinks of the city as Assyria's capital in the time of Jonah ben Amittai—a slight historical error, as Nineveh did not become Assyria's capital again until 705 under Sennacherib (cf. Hans Walter Wolff, *Obadiah and Jonah,* 99).

Jonah is to "cry against her" *(qara' 'al),* an unusual construction in Hebrew, *qara' el,* "to cry to," being much more common in pre-exilic Hebrew (cf. Athalja Brenner, "The Language of Jonah as an Index of Its Date," *Beth Mikra* 24 [1979]: 396-405 [in Hebrew], esp. p. 400; and the criticism of George M. Landes, "Linguistic Criteria and the Date of the Book of Jonah," *Eretz Israel* 16 [1982]: 147*-170*).

The "wickedness *(ra'ah)*" of Nineveh has come before God. One thinks immediately of the "outcry" against Sodom and Gomorrah and their very grave sin (Gen. 18:20). Our author paints a picture of Nineveh as a new Sodom. But the accusation of *ra'ah,* "wickedness," plays a most prominent part in Jeremiah's and Ezekiel's indictment against Jerusalem (Jer. 2:19; 4:18 [RSV "doom"]; 22:22; 23:11; 33:5; Ezek. 16:23). Jerusalem's wickedness has brought Yahweh's punishment upon it, according to Jeremiah and Ezekiel. The author of Jonah views the case of Nineveh in a similar light. (For the different meanings of *ra'ah* see Digression II on Jonah 4:1, pp. 114-117.)

3 And Jonah rises indeed, not to go to Nineveh, but to flee to Tarshish. It is not uncommon for an OT prophet to object to his commission. Jeremiah claims inability to speak on grounds of extreme youth (Jer. 1:6). But he is overcome by God's persuasion and reassurance (Jer. 1:7ff.). Jonah, obviously expecting similar treatment, just runs!

We do not know why Jonah is on the run. The narrator does not yet disclose Jonah's motives. He uses this technique to increase the tension of the narrative. Only *after* the encounter with the sailors, the journey back in the fish, and the conversion of the Ninevites will all be revealed in Jonah's outburst (Jonah 4:1-4).

But we do know in which direction he is heading: "to Tarshish, away from the presence of the LORD." I believe Eduard Haller (*Die Erzählung von dem Propheten Jona,* 15) coined the witticism: "Nach Nordosten soll er, nach Südwesten geht er"—while sent northeast, he is heading southwest! So, is Jonah just hell-bent on setting off in exactly the opposite direction? I think there is more to Tarshish, as can be seen from the added explanation "away from the LORD"! It is God he is running from—so why to Tarshish?

Tarshish is probably identical with the Iberian site, the later Greek colony Tartessos at the estuary of the river Guadalquivir in south-western Spain (cf. Herodotus *History* i.163) near modern Baetis. As such, it was beyond the Pillars of Hercules, on the very edge of the known world.

Already since ca. 800 and throughout the first half of the 8th cent. the Phoenicians seem to have sailed to southern Spain, according to Kurt Galling ("Der Weg der Phöniker nach Tarsis in literarischer und archäologischer Sicht," *ZDPV* 88 [1972]: 1-18, 140-181, esp. 180-81). "Ships of Tarshish" have almost become a naval boat class (cf. 1 Kgs. 22:48), the only ones suitable for the high seas. While voyages to Tarshish would have been quite a novelty at the time of Jonah ben Amittai, Phoenician ships still continued to travel from the Levant to Tarshish during the time of Persian supremacy (526-350), the suggested date for the book of Jonah. According to Galling, the Persian kings needed the Phoenician naval vessels from Tyre, Sidon, and Aradus in their struggle with the Greeks (at Salamis). Later the Persians did not interfere with the Phoenician western sea trade, as it filled the coffers of the Persian treasury.

It is to Tarshish that Jonah is fleeing from the presence of Yahweh. Clearly a panic decision! He could not really escape from his God by fleeing to Tarshish—and he knows it! When questioned by the sailors, he confesses his belief in Yahweh "who made the sea and the dry land" (Jonah 1:9). There is nowhere Jonah can escape, "away from the presence of the LORD." His very presence is everywhere.

Now Jonah *goes down* to Yaffo (Joppa) the harbor near modern Tel Aviv. Here in v. 3 begins Jonah's *continuous descent,* literally as well as symbolically (cf. Jonathan D. Magonet, *Form and Meaning,* 17). After having "gone down" to Yaffo, he pays his fare and "goes down" into the ship. When the storm breaks out he "goes down" into the innermost parts of the ship (v. 5). His descent continues in 2:6 when he "goes down" to the "roots of the mountains" (see below). So, by repeated use of the Hebrew verb *yarad,* "to go down," the author initiates a continuous downward movement as far as Jonah is concerned. This is obviously intended as contrast to the spiritual ascent of the pagans (sailors/Ninevites) who, from initial ignorance, are coming closer and closer to Yahweh.

Jonah goes to *Yaffo.* This is not a very likely choice for a man from Galilee, especially as he lives so close to the ports of Tyre and Sidon, from where the Phoenician Tarshish ships would have been sailing. But just as our author is not very interested in history, he is not very hot on geography either!

Jonah finds himself a *ship* going to Tarshish. The Hebrew word here is *aniyah* as opposed to *oniyah* in v. 4, but there does not appear to be any variance in meaning. He pays his fare (the Hebrew reads "her," the ship's fare) and continues to *go down* in the ship. He intends to travel with the sailors to Tarshish; and Tarshish, this verse repeats for the second time, means: *away from the presence of the LORD!*

So, while the section 1:1-3 begins with "the word of the LORD to Jonah," it ends with a double "away from the presence of the LORD"! Jonah's direction is clear, but his motives remain completely mysterious. Our narrator obviously wants to keep us on tenterhooks.

And apart from the direction *away*, Jonah also begins a movement *downwards*. To his intended flight from Yahweh corresponds his spiritual descent, which so far has brought him only on board ship, but which is ultimately to lead him to "the roots of the mountains." Distance from God and spiritual descent—it is in such notions that OT and NT anthropologies converge.

GOD'S RESPONSE
AND THE SAILORS' PERIL

1:4-6

---

4 After his initial command to the prophet, Yahweh had left all the reacting to Jonah. Now it is Yahweh's turn again. As he has all the forces of nature at his fingertips, he *throws* (Hebrew *hetil*) a *great* wind upon the sea, causing a *great* storm on it. Twice more the author's favorite Hebrew word *gadol* appears, adding wind and storm to the *great* city. Yahweh is using his big guns right away, with the effect that the ship threatens to break up.

5 This now places the pagan sailors in the position of innocent victims of the struggle, Yahweh versus Jonah. The author obviously invites our sympathy with the sailors—thereby attacking Jonah indirectly (cf. John C. Holbert, "'Deliverance belongs to Yahweh!': Satire in the Book of Jonah," *JSOT* 21 [1981]: 70).

The sailors *are afraid* (Hebrew *yare*). This is the first word in vv. 5, 10, and 16. "To fear" is obviously a key word in ch. 1. So far the sailors are "only" afraid; but different kinds of "fear" are to come. For the time being, the sailors express their fear by crying "each to his god." Our Phoenician (?) Tarshish ship is obviously served by an international crew, a collection of pagans each of whom cries to his own god. No value judgment is passed on this act of the pagan sailors. The author takes this to be a natural response. But the sailors also take practical steps: they make the ship lighter by *throwing* the cargo overboard (cf. Acts 27:18-19, 38). The verb *hetil* is used, as for Yahweh's "throwing" of the great wind (Jonah 1:4).

Only one person does not join in: Jonah, the Hebrew (v. 9). While our attention has been focused on the mariners, we are now told what he has been up to in the meantime. He has continued his *descent* by "going down" *(yarad)* to the innermost parts of the ship to avoid being seasick. The word for ship this time is *sephinah*. Again there seems to be no real difference of meaning.

Having reached the lowest point on board ship, Jonah lies down and *goes to sleep* (Hebrew *niredam*). The same root is used for man's "complete anesthetic" in Gen. 2:21 for the purpose of removing one of his ribs. (I owe this remark to Hans Walter Wolff, whose Jonah seminar in Heidelberg during the summer semester 1975 I was privileged to attend.) Jonah goes to sleep, not caring for his own life nor that of the sailors. His direction is still "away from the LORD," come what may.

6 The captain, a shrewd man, has become suspicious and now approaches this strange passenger. He is outraged by Jonah's sleep and wakes him up. And now—O wonderful irony!—Jonah hears again the same command that he had chosen to ignore earlier on: "arise, cry *(qum qera)*!" Those had been Yahweh's words in v. 2. It is now *to* his God that the captain wants him to call.

Why does the captain want him to call to his God? At this point the captain is still in complete ignorance of who this God might be. However, he wants to try all possible avenues. Perhaps Jonah's God will spare them a thought—whoever he may be! The same "perhaps" (Hebrew *ulay*) also turns up in the king of Nineveh's calculation: *Perhaps (mi-yodeaʿ)* the deity will repent (3:9).

In both cases we find the same cryptic reference to *the deity (ha'elohim)*, as neither the pagan captain nor the pagan king know who this God is, who is threatening disaster. They also both express hope "that we do not perish *(welo' no 'bed)*" (1:6//3:9). The verb *abad*, "to perish," is also a key word in the book of Jonah. Apart from the two passages already mentioned, it occurs in 1:14 in the mariners' prayer "let us not perish" and in the reference to "the plant . . . which . . . perished in a night" (4:10).

The root *abad* therefore establishes two parallels: that between the sailors and the Ninevites, and that between Nineveh and the plant, the latter being an example for the former. We may already note the following parallels between 1:4-6 and ch. 3: the captain's role on board ship corresponds to that of the king of Nineveh; they both hold out hope ("perhaps"), hope "that (they) may not perish," even if they are still ignorant of "the deity." From the parallels between mariners and Ninevites it should be obvious that the *Gentiles* play an important part in the book of Jonah. Whether this is in opposition to *Israel* should become clear in the following scene, 1:7-10.

So far Yahweh's intervention has led to the involvement of a third party, the mariners. Their captain discovers Jonah; and ironically, it is he, the pagan, who repeats Yahweh's command to Jonah: "Arise, cry"! While Jonah is asleep, not caring for his own life or that of any other person, the mariners cry each to his god that they may not perish! We are never told that Jonah responded to the captain's plea. While we are meant to sympathize with the sailors, Jonah is painted in almost repulsive colors. As Abraham is outdone in his fear of God by the pagan king Abimelech (Gen. 20), so is the prophet Jonah, by a crew of pagan sailors. We may note the honesty of the OT in both cases (cf. Matt. 12:41 for the NT).

THE CULPRIT IDENTIFIED
1:7-10

7 While the captain may have had a pretty shrewd idea about his strange passenger, a more reliable method of investigation is called for. Lots are suggested as a means of identifying the culprit (*beshellemi*, "on whose account," is very late Hebrew!), and lots it is. The importance and solemnity of the occasion is conveyed to us by the threefold repetition within one verse: "Let us cast lots," "so they cast lots," and "the lot fell upon Jonah"—the verbs "to cast" and "to fall" coming from the same Hebrew root.

8 So now *Jonah* is identified as the cause of the disaster that has befallen the ship and its crew. And now the questioning begins. Five questions are put to Jonah:
1. "On whose account has this evil (Hebrew *ra'ah*; cf. Digression II on 4:1) come upon us?"
2. "What is your occupation?"
3. "Whence do you come?"
4. "What is your country?"
5. "Of what people are you?"

These are all leading questions; the real question, "What is wrong between you and your God?" is never asked—though at least the captain must have guessed intuitively *where*, though not *what*, the problem was.

9 Jonah then proceeds to answer *some* of the questions. The answer to question 1 is really self-evident. The lot has already identified Jonah as the culprit. Yet the fair-minded mariners—and our narrator means us to notice how fair-minded they are!—are looking to Jonah to confirm what the lot has already indicated. His silence is an admission of guilt.

Question 2 (occupation) is equally embarrassing for Jonah. How could he have replied: "I am a prophet of Yahweh, presently engaged in running away from my mission"? So again, Jonah chooses to remain silent.

But he does provide answers to questions 3-5, not only to the questions as they have been worded, but also to the real issue behind them: his *religion*! The sailors were far too polite (or afraid?) to attack this issue directly, but Jonah understands their questions just the same, and he answers openly.

First, he confesses to being a *Hebrew*, what Schalom ben-Chorin calls the Jewish *Urbekenntnis*, which is both self-awareness and the most basic public confession (*Die Antwort des Jona zum Gestaltwandel Israels*, 14). Now the position of our author is clear; he confronts the Gentiles, represented by a pagan multinational crew of mariners, with Jonah, the *Hebrew*. It is now no longer possible to eliminate the subject "Jews and Gentiles," as traditional Jewish exegesis has done, e.g., the medieval commentator David Kimchi (1160?-1235?). Jonah 1:9 contradicts Elias J. Bickerman's statement: "The opposition between Israel and the Gentiles is introduced by commentators who find more than is really there" (*Four Strange Books of the Bible*, 28).

Jonah secondly confesses to being a Yahweh worshipper, and he describes Yahweh as "the God of heaven" *(elohe hashshamayim)*. "The God of heaven" is the common Persian clerical reference to the God of the Jews. The Cyrus edict, quoted in Ezra 1:2-4, states: "Thus says Cyrus king of Persia: The LORD, the God of heaven, has given me all the kingdoms of the earth, and he has charged me to build him a house at Jerusalem, which is in Judah" (v. 2//2 Chr. 36:23). When Nehemiah hears of the sorry state of Jerusalem, he weeps and prays to "the God of heaven" (Neh. 1:4-5). Nehemiah is probably writing for readers at the Persian court, hence the strange title (cf. also Neh. 2:4, 20, and elsewhere).

These passages in Chronicles/Ezra/Nehemiah suggest to me that Jonah 1:9 also must be attributed to the Persian period. There are, however, two completely isolated references to "the God of heaven" in Gen. 24:3, 7, in Abraham's instructions to the servant who is to find a wife for Isaac. As the existence of pentateuchal sources and their possible dating has become an open question again (at least since Rolf Rendtorff, *Das überlieferungsgeschichtliche Problem des Pentateuch),* the simplest solution would be to attribute Gen. 24 to the Persian period. Further support for this suggestion comes from the occurrences of "the God of heaven" in Aramaic (Dan. 2:37 and elsewhere).

This God of heaven "made the sea and the dry land." Jonah knows this from his religious tradition, but he has obviously not taken it into account. What was the point of trying to flee from the

God "who made the sea" in a Tarshish ship? Hans Walter Wolff (*Obadiah and Jonah*, 115) points to the fact that the *sea* is deliberately mentioned before the land! Jonah fails to apply in practice what he knows from his religious tradition. The same is true of the "psalm" (Jonah 2) and of his statement in 4:2 that Yahweh is a "gracious God." He knows this, but fails to relate it to the Ninevites in the same way as he had failed to relate his earlier statement to the sailors. Here again the fate of the mariners and that of the Ninevites are exactly parallel (against Bickermann). Failure to understand is quite different from *hypocrisy*. Only an anti-Jewish exegesis would charge the prophet with the latter (cf. my article, "Jonaexegese und Antijudaismus," *Kirche und Israel* [1986], 51-61).

10   And now the men are "exceedingly afraid." The first word of v. 10 takes up the first word of v. 5 *(wayyire'u)*. While v. 5 simply says "they feared," v. 10 adds "a great fear," and v. 16 "to the LORD." This is what Jonathan D. Magonet (*Form and Meaning*, 31-33) calls a *growing phrase*:

  v. 5   "they feared"
  v. 10   "they feared a great fear"
  v. 16   "they feared a great fear to the LORD."

(Cf. Gabriel Hayim Cohn, *Das Buch Jona im Lichte der biblischen Erzählkunst*, 53; and Digression I on 1:16). This deliberate use of the "growing phrase" signals the increase in the sailors' feelings. While the storm as such—so terrible was it—already filled them, the professionals, with fear, this new revelation sends them into absolute horror: Here is a human being trying to challenge his God!

The mariners repeat their first question "What is this that you have done"? But again they get no answer. The sailors persist in questioning Jonah, "for the men knew"—and I should say, instinctively!—"that he was fleeing from the presence of the LORD." Instinctively, and not "because (Jonah) had told them." Jonah never does reveal why he is fleeing from Yahweh. He simply confesses to being a Yahweh *worshipper*. But the mariners grasp quite intuitively where the problem lies, and the false explanation that "he had told them" must be a glossator's error. This glossator underestimated the mariners and provided a rather too simplistic explanation (against Wolff, *Obadiah and Jonah*, 117, who accepts the explanation of 1:10).

Our narrator has now completed the second and third stages of the proceedings. After Jonah's flight Yahweh has taken countermeasures, the great storm. This has led to the involvement of a third party, the mariners, who become the innocent victims of Jonah's disobedience. The mariners have now identified Jonah as the source of their trouble. In questioning Jonah they have been fair to him who, by his behavior, has been extremely unfair to them. However, as their lives are at risk, there must be a solution to this intolerable situation. Where is it going to come from?

THE SOLUTION AND ITS
UNEXPECTED CONSEQUENCES
1:11-16

11 As Jonah is the only person who understands completely the "ins" and "outs" of their situation, the mariners do the only logical thing by turning to him for advice: By what means can this storm be brought to an end?

12 "Take me up and *throw* me into the sea," advises Jonah.loong Again the key verb *hetil* is used. In v. 4 Yahweh "threw" a great wind upon the sea. Then it was the sailors' turn to do the "throwing" (v. 5). But the "throwing" of the cargo provided only temporary relief. Now Jonah advises (v. 12) that he ought to be "thrown," and when his advice is carried out (v. 15, again *hetil*) the desired result is achieved.

If Jonah is thrown overboard, the sea will become calm. And Jonah now confesses that "it is because of me that this great tempest has come upon you." This is Jonah's first partial *confession*. It is not very easy for the expositor to evaluate correctly Jonah's confession and the offer of his own life. For anti-Jewish exegesis this is just stubbornness: Jonah would rather die than obey Yahweh's command and carry out his mission to Nineveh. The opposite view paints a picture of Jonah as the "suffering servant" who gives his life for others: "The drama of Jonah is interpreted in terms of the 'servitude' of the prophet" (Carl A. Keller, "Jonas: Le portrait d'un prophète," *ThZ* 21 [1965]: 329-340, esp. 339).

Perhaps the truth lies somewhere in the middle. It is not easy to dismiss the "stubbornness" argument completely, because Jonah's death wish reappears in connection with Nineveh (4:3, 8)—another parallel between sailors and Ninevites! On the other hand, Jonah realizes for the first time that he is putting other people in grave danger, and his ensuing sacrifice has the desired effect. The fact that he does not actually die is neither here nor there. Yahweh has means of keeping Jonah alive, because he has no "pleasure in the death of the wicked" but would "rather that he should turn from his way and live" (Ezek. 18:23).

13   But no, Jonah's offer is not accepted—yet! The author goes on painting his picture of the worthy pagans. Before sacrificing Jonah, they are trying to row as hard as they can to return the ship "to the dry land" *(el-hayyabbashah)*—to no avail because it is not the ship, but Jonah whom Yahweh wants returned! The big fish vomits Jonah *el-hayyabbashah* quite unceremoniously (Jonah 2:10). In the meantime, the mariners try harder and harder—but so does the sea by growing "more and more tempestuous against them."

14   It now seems only a matter of time before Jonah is to go overboard. But before the mariners resort to this ultimate solution, they cry *(qara')* to Yahweh, whom they now know to be the deity responsible for the great storm. The same verb *qara'* is used in Yahweh's command to Jonah: "Cry against it" (v. 2). But it would appear that the pagans are rather better at it.

They beg Yahweh not to let them *perish*—again the key verb *abad* (cf. 1:6; 3:9; 4:10)—"for this man's life." Yahweh is not to place "innocent" blood upon them. This means that the mariners pray that they should not become *guilty* by sacrificing Jonah. Hans Walter Wolff has perfectly understood the satire involved in this verse by contrasting 1:14 with Jer. 26:15: "There a true prophet warns a wicked people (Jerusalem!) against shedding his innocent blood. Here good non-Israelites, who are face to face with a prophet who is not good at all, pray that they should not acquire guilt through his death" *(Obadiah and Jonah,* 120). Only satire can change traditional roles around in this way, the purpose being the instruction of the reader.

The conclusion of Jonah 1:14, applied to Yahweh, sounds like good polytheistic coinage with which the pagan sailors would have been familiar: You are the god X; you have done as it pleased you! In this case the mariners are keen to emphasize the fact that their present situation is not of their own making. They are only the innocent victims of the struggle, Yahweh versus Jonah.

15   After all human possibilities have been exhausted and religious precautions have been taken, the time has come to dispatch Jonah into the sea. The sailors lift him up and *throw* him in *(wayetiluhu,* again the verb *hetil*). After wind and cargo, this is the final throw!

And now something *fantastic* happens: The sea is calmed *instantly.* According to Leonard Feinberg, *Introduction to Satire,* the fantastic is one of the characteristics of satire. This has been identified in the book of Jonah by John C. Holbert ("'Deliverance

Belongs to Yahweh!'" 62, 69-70). And how do the pagan sailors react to this fantastic spectacle that takes place in front of their own eyes?

16 They simply turn to Yahweh, whom they now know to be the Lord of the storm and the sea, in worship and adoration. This must be the most solemn verse of the OT, first through its use of the "growing phrase." It takes up v. 5 again: "(The men) feared," and v. 10: "a great fear," and now adds: "to Yahweh." With the use of this "growing phrase" our narrator contrasts the *three fears*. The panic of v. 5 and the absolute horror in the light of Jonah's awesome confession (v. 10) have found a solution in the "fear" that transcends all "fears," the worship of Yahweh.

Second, this is probably the only verse in the OT expressing the solemnity of the occasion by a threefold use of the *figura etymologica*. Jonah 1 concludes: "And the men *feared* a great *fear* of the LORD, they *sacrificed sacrifices* to the LORD, and they *vowed vows*." Surely in English we should say "they were *overcome* by a great fear, they *offered* sacrifices, and they *made* vows." While we try to avoid a repetition of the same stem in verb and noun, the Hebrew—and occasionally NT Greek—delights in that very repetition. This procedure, *figura etymologica*, an "etymological figure," implies that a verb is followed by an object noun from the same stem: to dream dreams, to offer offerings, to fear a fear, to vow a vow, to sin sins, to devise devices. While it would be perfectly possible to say "to offer offerings" or "to sacrifice sacrifices," English uses a bastard construction, "to offer sacrifices"—half Germanic, half Latin—in order to avoid the *figura etymologica* at all costs.

So, were the Hebrews just clumsy because they resorted so frequently to this device? I have counted more than four hundred occurrences of it in the OT! My main witness against this assumption is the so-called Succession narrative (2 Sam. 9-20; 1 Kgs. 1-2), the story of Solomon's eventual succession to the throne of David. This narrative is commonly regarded as a masterpiece of Hebrew language, literature, and psychology (Jan P. Fokkelman, *Narrative Art and Poetry in the Books of Samuel,* 1: *King David*). The Succession narrative has seventeen occurrences and uses eleven different *figurae etymologicae,* some unique or almost unique in the OT!

My second witness is the ancient story of the ark (1 Sam. 4-6; 2 Sam. 6). There are eight occurrences, involving six different *figurae etymologicae*—and that in a mere four chapters! Another pearl of Hebrew storytelling is the Joseph story (Gen. 37–50). While there are only five *figurae* in use—mainly Joseph dreaming dreams!—the number of occurrences (eighteen) tops even the Succession narrative. And finally our book of Jonah itself: six different *figurae* and seven occurrences in only forty-eight verses! Two of them, "to fear a fear" and "to cry a cry" ("to proclaim a message") are unique in the OT. Jonah 1:16, quoted above, displays three *figurae* in one verse! Surely, this must be quite deliberate.

We therefore have two solutions in this section, a permanent one: The storm has been calmed instantly by Jonah's sacrifice, and a preliminary one: The word of Yahweh has reached the pagans—"but they are the *wrong* pagans" (Holbert, 66)! One thinks of the prophet of the Babylonian exile, the Second Isaiah, who says of the word of Yahweh: "It shall not return to me empty, but it shall accomplish that which I purpose, and prosper in the thing for which I sent it" (Isa. 55:11). The purpose here was clearly the conversion of the Gentiles.

The motif of God-fearing pagans is not uncommon in the OT. In Gen. 20 Abimelech, king of Gerar, surpasses Abraham's fear of God. In Exod. 1:15-21 the Egyptian midwives to the Hebrew women ignore Pharaoh's command to kill the Hebrew boys (cf. Brevard S. Childs, *The Book of Exodus,* 17). "And because the midwives feared God he gave them families" (Exod. 1:21). And there is the Edomite (?) Job, the man from the land of Uz "who feared God, and turned away from evil" (Job 1:1; cf. vv. 8-9).

This is the point where the element of the grotesque enters the book of Jonah: "Pagans worshipping Yahweh while Yahweh's prophet seeks for ultimate escape from him" (Holbert, 70). Jonah, who is fleeing from his commission and his God, nevertheless becomes an instrument of the conversion of the sailors to Yahweh. In this he foreshadows Peter, who thrice denies Christ and yet becomes "the rock."

But the issue of the correct pagan addressees of the word of Yahweh is still unresolved. Nineveh is still persisting in its wickedness (*ra'ah*) and awaiting Jonah's message. Is the city to be disappointed?

A STRANGE PRAYER
FROM THE BELLY OF THE FISH

1:17–2:10

This is the only section where the numbering of verses in the RSV disagrees with the Hebrew text (RSV 1:17 = Hebrew 2:1; in ch. 2 add 1 to the RSV numbering to get the Hebrew equivalent).

1:17 Nineveh is not to be disappointed. Yahweh takes action by starting a series of "appointments" in the book. He *appoints* (Hebrew *wayeman*) a great fish. There are more "appointments" to come in ch. 4: the plant, 4:6; the worm, v. 7; and the sultry east wind, v. 8. Hebrew *wayeman* is another key word indicating the superiority of the Creator over his creation (cf. Job 38–41). Almost playfully God "appoints" fish, plant, worm, and wind in order to move the action in the required direction.

Yahweh's first "appointment" is a *great fish*—again the key word *gadol*: after the great city, wind, storm, and fear, now the great fish! No species is named—there is no whale in the book of Jonah! Commentators of former ages have spent much time and paper debating in which species Jonah could have survived for three days and three nights. The fish is simply a fantasy fish, big enough to provide transport and shelter for Jonah. This motif is just as fantastic as the instant calming of the sea (Jonah 1:15).

Perhaps the great fish also provides the answer to the mention of the unlikely Yaffo as Jonah's port of embarkation (v. 3). Tales of sea monsters were common on the Levantine coast, and it is not impossible for one such story to have been located or transmitted at Yaffo. According to Hans Walter Wolff (*Studien zum Jonabuch*, 24), the big fish resembles the sea monsters of the Heracles and Perseus sagas. Sent by Poseidon, it threatens Hesione (who is tied to a rock) and Andromeda, respectively. The two heroes kill the monster by climbing into its throat. I wonder, however, whether these sagas really have anything to do with Jonah's fish. For a start, the fish is no hostile monster that has to be killed, but a friendly means of transport at Yahweh's command; and Jonah, by Jove, is no hero—rather, he is an anti-hero, if ever there was one! The big fish *swallows* Jonah just as unceremoniously as the mariners dispatch him. Jonah has lost the initiative; he has become totally passive. But he has "three days and three nights" "in the belly of the fish" to ponder his situation and to regain the initiative.

The "three days and three nights" were understood by the early Church (Matt. 12:40; Jerome; Cyril of Alexandria) as prefiguring Christ in the tomb. But the analogy is not a very precise one, Jonah exceeding Jesus' stay by at least one night!

More promising is the analogy between the *belly* of the fish and the womb of the mythical *great mother*. In this case, Jonah's stay in the belly of the fish has its mythical counterpart in the rites of rebirth (cf. Uwe Steffen, *Jona und der Fisch: Der Mythos von Tod und Wiedergeburt,* 109-130). But here, too, caution is necessary. Whether Jonah has really been changed or just forced into submission is an open question.

2:1 However, Jonah is taking a step in the right direction by praying "to the LORD his God from the belly of the fish." *His* God has a slightly ironic ring about it after Jonah's desertion and the enthusiastic conversion of the mariners to Yahweh, accompanied by sacrifices, with more vowed for the future (1:16).

In 2:2-9 follows Jonah's prayer, the so-called Jonah "psalm."

DIGRESSION I
The Authorship of the Jonah "Psalm"

Before we consider the question whether the Jonah psalm in ch. 2 is to be attributed to the author of the narrative or to a later editor of the book, let us be quite clear on whose side the onus of proof lies in this argument. The canonical text of the book of Jonah that we have before us wishes to be understood as a continuous story, including a prayer of the prophet from the belly of the fish, all written by one and the same author. This is the way the book must be understood unless there are *compelling reasons* for assuming a multiplicity of authorship. I repeat, the onus of proof lies on the side of the critics of the book's unity—not on the side of its defenders. If the arguments hang in the balance, the critical case must be considered unproven.

On the whole, source criticism seems to have gone out of fashion—with perhaps the exception of Germany, where the spirit of

Julius Wellhausen is raising its head again and more refined literary subdivisions are being prepared even today. However, the trend of international scholarship elsewhere has certainly been to understand a biblical text in the first instance as we find it, unless there are good reasons to the contrary—as a "reconstructed" text is always easier to interpret than the actual one.

Similarly in the case of the book of Jonah, G. H. Cohn and Jonathan D. Magonet have made out a strong case for the unity of the book. And one might well have regarded this issue as closed, were it not for the fact that the most important Jonah commentary of the last ten years, Wolff's *Obadiah and Jonah,* reverts to the "critical" position with even more recent support from Juan Alberto Soggin ("Il 'segno del Giona' nel libro del profeta Giona," *Lateranum* 48 [1982]: 70-74).

Soggin makes much of the fact that the Song of Hannah (1 Sam. 2) and the Psalm of Hezekiah (Isa. 38:9-20; omitted in the parallel text, 2 Kgs. 20) are generally regarded as secondary. But does this really have any bearing on Jonah? Soggin asserts that the author of the psalm wants Jonah to "convert" in the same way as the sailors and the Ninevites have done; on the hermeneutical level, the psalm allegedly provides the key for our reading of the whole book (Soggin, 74).

However, Soggin never discusses the possibility of an ironic significance of the psalm that might enable us to hold on to the unity of the book. While his own interpretation is attractive, the case for the secondary nature of the psalm remains unproven.

Wolff argues, first, that the *situation* presupposed by the psalm does not fit the context, which means the psalm, as a Song of Thanksgiving, is inappropriate at this place. It would fit the temple better than the belly of the fish (Wolff, *Obadiah and Jonah,* 129).

However, even on Wolff's own terms, this argument does not really solve the problem. The "inappropriateness" is the same whether we regard the author of the narrative or a later editor of the book as the author of the psalm. Or is Wolff taking an editor for such a complete fool that he would not have noticed the "inappropriateness"?

But is the psalm really "inappropriate"? A straight reading taking the text at face value might suggest this. But as Magonet (*Form and Meaning,* 49-54) has shown, "the apparent 'inappropriateness' of the psalm disappears if one recognises the ironic purpose it fulfils in the book, like the other pious citations and prayers of Jonah" (54). So, there is a perfectly satisfactory way of understanding the psalm in its present context—i.e., the "inappropriateness" argument is not compelling.

Wolff contends, second, that the *language* of the psalm is different from that of the story. By far the strongest point in Wolff's favor is his observation that the author's favorite word *gadol,* "great," occurs fourteen times in thirty-nine narrative verses, but never in the psalm (Wolff, 129). Is this not a sure indication of different authorship?

The usage of *gadol* in the book of Jonah is confined to three areas:

(1) *Stereotyped references to Nineveh,* "that great city" (Jonah 1:2; 3:2-3; 4:11); and within Nineveh its leading citizens, "the great ones" (3:5, 7).

(2) *References to God's actions* involving a "great wind" (1:4), a "great tempest" (vv. 4, 12), and a "great fish" (v. 17).

(3) *References to human psychological conditions*: the "great fear" of the sailors (1:10, 16) and Jonah's "great *ra'ah* ("displeasure" or "wickedness"?)" (4:1) as well as his "great joy" (v. 6).

The dimension of the *"greatness"* of Nineveh in the narrative is replaced by that of *"depth"* in the psalm. Jonah is cast "into the heart of the seas" (2:3), he is "at the roots of the mountains" (v. 6), and he goes "down to the land whose bars closed upon (him) for ever" (v. 6). The depth represents Jonah's distance from God.

Corresponding to this, the *greatness* of God's actions (wind, storm, fish) is replaced by the image of *"height."* God "brings" Jonah "up from the Pit" (v. 6). This is traditional psalm language: "Who is seated on high" and "looks far down" (Ps. 113:5-6); "The LORD looks down from heaven, he sees all the sons of men; from where he sits enthroned he looks forth on all the inhabitants of the earth" (Ps. 33:13-14). In individual Songs of Thanksgiving the depth/height imagery predominates; it is in the more abstract descriptive praise that we hear of the greatness of God's acts (Ps. 95:3ff.; 145:3ff.; 150).

The psychological conditions in the book of Jonah are always stated in 3rd person narrative using the *figura etymologica*. I do not know of a psalm where the worshipper speaks of himself as "fearing a great fear" or "joying a great joy" to the Lord. Occurrences of *gadol,* "great" involving psychological conditions are therefore not to be expected in the Jonah psalm.

Reviewing the three areas of the usage of *gadol* in the book of Jonah, we are perhaps no longer quite so surprised by its absence in the psalm, and Wolff's argument thus loses much of its force. Hence the absence of *gadol* in the psalm raises no questions of authorship.

But of course, Wolff is quite right when he observes a difference between the language of the narrative and that of the psalm (Wolff, 129). The Jonah psalm has been created on purpose by the book's author through the use of bits and pieces from the Psalter, as Magonet (44-49) has shown. This language is quite deliberately traditional, reminding the readers of their prayer book. The psalm is ironic insofar as Jonah uses pious language out of concern for himself, but has not one word of regret about his failure to carry out his mission to Nineveh.

Following Magonet's diagram (50), I shall try to give the cross references between the Jonah psalm and the Psalter.

Jonah 2		**Psalter**	
2	I called to the LORD out of my distress, and he answered me;	120:1	I cry to the LORD . . . in my distress . . . that he may answer me:
	out of the belly of Sheol I cried, and thou didst hear my voice.	31:22b	. . . when I cried to thee for help . . . but thou didst hear my supplications . . .
3	For thou didst cast me	102:10	. . . thou hast . . . thrown me away.
	into the deep,	69:2	I have come into deep waters,
	into the heart of the seas, and the flood was round about me;		and the flood sweeps over me.
	all thy waves and thy billows passed over me.	42:7	. . . all thy waves and thy billows have gone over me.
4	Then I said,	31:22a	I had said in my alarm,
	"I am cast out from thy presence;		"I am driven far from thy sight."
	how shall I again look upon thy temple?"	5:7	I will worship toward thy holy temple.
5	The waters closed in over me,	9:1	For the waters have come up to my neck.
	the deep was round about me; weeds were wrapped about my head	18:4	. . . the torrents of perdition assailed me . . . The cords of death encompassed me . . .

6	at the roots of the mountains. I went down to the land whose bars closed upon me for ever;		
	yet thou didst bring up my life from the Pit, O LORD my God.	103:4	. . . who redeems your life from the Pit . . .
7	When my soul fainted within me,	142:3	When my spirit is faint . . .
	I remember the LORD;	143:5	I remember the days of old . . .
	and my prayer came to thee, into thy holy temple.	88:2	Let my prayer come before thee, incline thy ear to my cry!
8	Those who pay regard to vain idols forsake their true loyalty.	31:6	Thou hatest those who pay regard to vain idols; but I trust in the LORD.
9	But I with the voice of thanksgiving will sacrifice to thee;	116:17	I will offer thee the sacrifice of thanks- giving . . .
	what I have vowed I will pay.	116:18	I will pay my vows to the LORD . . .
	Deliverance belongs to the LORD!	3:8	Deliverance belongs to the LORD . . .

Using pious language, Jonah is nevertheless still silent on the subject of Nineveh and his own desertion.

Wolff's third and final argument, that the Jonah of the psalm is a different *person* from the one of the story (Wolff, 130), stands or falls with the other two. If the meaning of the psalm is *ironic,* then Jonah's person is "quite consistent in its inner problematic with the character ascribed to Jonah throughout the book" (Magonet, 54).

It would therefore appear that none of Wolff's three objections (situation, language, person) are really compelling. As different authorship for the psalm still remains unproven, we shall proceed with our exegesis of ch. 2 on the assumption of the unity of the book.

---

2 *"I called"* (Hebrew *qara'ti*) is how Jonah begins his Song of Thanksgiving. While v. 2a is virtually identical with Ps. 120:1, the position of *qara'ti* is significantly different. Psalm 120 begins with "to the LORD"; Jonah begins with "I"! In fact Jonah 2:2, 4, 9 begin with "I," vv. 3, 5 with "me." If the psalmist is Yahweh-orientated, Jonah is still as self-centered as ever. The very first word of Jonah's psalm confirms the continuity between narrative and psalm: we are dealing with one and the same person (against Wolff, 130).

But *cry (qara')* he does. What Yahweh (1:2) and the captain (v. 6) failed to achieve with their commands, Jonah now does quite voluntarily *in his distress*! This is what he is concerned with—not with his desertion and the fate of Nineveh.

"And Yahweh *answered me*," continues Jonah with Ps. 120. As a matter of fact, the answer, in the form of the big fish was ready and waiting for him, before he could even ask for it. But how is Jonah going to answer when Yahweh next calls him?

He cries "out of the belly of *Sheol*." Sheol is a nonplace in the concept of the Hebrews. It has no real existence, because the dead do not praise Yahweh (Ps. 6:5; 30:9; 88:11-12; Isa. 38:18-19; Ps. 115:17; 118:17; 119:175; Sir. 17:27-28; cf. Claus Westermann, *Praise and Lament in the Psalms,* 155-161). Life in the OT is praise, life before God. Death means simply distance from God. Jonah, although physically still alive, is nevertheless in Sheol because he has cut himself off from Yahweh (cf. Cain in Gen. 4:1-16). Yet God hears his voice.

3 "For thou didst *cast* me." The familiar motif of *throwing* (wind, cargo, Jonah) continues in the psalm. But, as Jonah is using traditional language, the *hetil* of Jonah 1:4 , 5, 12, 15 has been changed for the verb *hishlik* under the influence of Ps. 102:10.

"Into the deep" *(metsulah)* has a parallel in Ps. 69:2. It is part of the technique of our author to let the original situation of the psalmists shine through in the Jonah psalm (Magonet, 54). Psalm 69, an Individual Lament, is a particularly instructive example.

> Save me, O God!
> For the waters have come up to my neck.
> I sink in deep mire,
> where there is no foothold;
> I have come into deep waters,
> and the flood sweeps over me.
> I am weary with my crying;
> my throat is parched.
> My eyes grow dim
> with waiting for my God. (vv. 1-3)

This Individual Lament (readers not familiar with the basic forms of psalms should refer to Westermann, *Praise and Lament*) represents Jonah's situation quite accurately. By quoting *metsulah* to Jews familiar with their prayer book, the author of Jonah evokes like an "echo" (Magonet, 54) the situation of a familiar Individual Lament.

"Into the heart of the seas" is unparalleled in the Psalter, but "and the flood was round about me" continues the quotation from Ps. 69:2.

"All thy waves and thy billows passed over me" quotes verbatim the Hebrew of Ps. 42:7b. Ps. 42 has the style of a Hebrew *qinah,* a death lament (cf. Hans-Joachim Kraus, *Psalmen 1-59*). With this phrase our author takes up again the earlier *Sheol* motif (Jonah 2:2).

4 "Then I said"—again Jonah's "I," emphasized in Hebrew *wa'ani—"I am cast out from thy presence."* While this half verse—with the addition of "in my alarm"—has an immediate parallel in Ps. 31:22a, we are also reminded of *Cain* and the Sheol motif.

> Behold, thou has driven me this day away from the ground;
> and from thy face I shall be hidden;
> and I shall be a fugitive and a wanderer on the earth,
> and whoever finds me will slay me. (Gen. 4:14)

Jonah, like Cain, has become one of the desperate people in the OT, in total confrontation with God, driven from his presence. While Cain goes far away from the presence of his God, Jonah—having failed to do that (!)—is thrown "into the deep," into Sheol, the nonplace.

How shall he "again look upon thy holy *temple*"? The temple in question is the one in Jerusalem. While at the time of Jonah ben Amittai the Jerusalem temple would not have been the *only* legitimate sanctuary—for we are still more than a hundred years before Josiah's reform (622 B.C.) (2 Kgs. 22–23)—this is certainly the case at the time of the author of Jonah. At this point, of course, we are talking about the Second Temple. Whether Ps. 5, to which Jonah now alludes, is pre- or postexilic is impossible to decide (cf. Kraus, 175-76). Psalm 5 is an Individual Lament in which the "foe lament" (Westermann) is particularly prominent. The psalmist will enter the house of God and "worship toward thy holy temple" (Ps. 5:7b). This is in deliberate contrast to the situation of Jonah, who through his flight "away from the presence of the LORD" is prevented from doing just that.

5 For "the waters closed in over me"; cf. again the parallel in Ps. 69:1: "For the waters have come up to my neck." "The *deep* was round about me." The great deep *(tehom)* appears in the first chapter of our Bible (Gen. 1:2 "Darkness was upon the face of the deep").

According to Westermann *(Genesis 1-11,* 105), *tehom* occurs thirty-five times in the OT, always with the meaning "flood (of waters)." It has lost any mythical allusion to the Babylonian goddess Tiamat (cf. Alexander Heidel, *The Babylonian Genesis).* The OT uses *tehom* often in connection with creation and also where blessing and providing is concerned. But the passages that concern us in connection with Jonah 2:5 are those referring to *tehom* as a threatening and *destructive* flood (e.g., Gen. 7:11; 8:2; Exod. 15:8; Ps. 36:6; 71:20; 106:9; 107:26; Isa. 51:10; 63:13; Ezek. 26:19; Amos 7:4). Floods of water are threatening Jonah. His only protection is the great fish, appointed by Yahweh.

Reeds—not "weeds" (as the RSV has it!)—are wrapped around Jonah's head. The Reed Sea *(yam suph)* is often identified with *tehom* and vice versa (Exod. 15:5, 8; Ps. 106:9; Isa. 51:10; 63:13). The meaning of all three parts (waters, the deep, "reeds") is therefore the same: Jonah is threatened by great primeval floods, but he is protected from them by Yahweh like his ancestors, the Exodus group (Exod. 15:8). For this verse cf. also Ps. 18:4.

6 Verse 6a has no parallel in the Psalter. It is the author's own creation, linked to the narrative by the key verb *yarad,* "to go down." Jonah continues his *descent:* He goes down to Yaffo and into the ship (1:3); during the storm he descends into the innermost parts of the ship (v. 5) for protection from the storm; now he has gone down to the roots of the mountains inside the great fish.

However, this is not entirely clear from the RSV translation, which is in error in linking "at the roots of the mountains" to the previous verse—which requires a change from *le,* "to," to *be,* "at." Such liberties with the Hebrew text are not permissible when it makes perfect sense as it stands:

> To the roots of the mountains I went down,
> —the earth *(ha'arets—casus pendens)*
> —its bars closed upon me for ever!

Or in plain English:

> I went down to the roots of the mountains;
> the bars of the earth closed upon me for ever.

Verse 6a is our author's special creation. Continuing his descent (*yarad*), Jonah reaches literally "rock bottom" in the psalm. He is still self-centered and not yet ready for his commission. So far Psalter language was sufficient; here words fail our author and he must create them himself!

6b This verse represents the turning point of the psalm. Psalter language recommences when Yahweh brings Jonah up "from the Pit" (Psalm 103:4: "Who redeems your life from the Pit"). Jonah 2:6b uses *he'elah*, "to bring up," in contrast to Jonah's "going down" (*yarad*, 1:3, 5; 2:6a). Psalm 103:4 has *ga'al*, "to redeem" (*go'el*, "who redeems"). This plainly echoes two of Jonah's theological predecessors, Deutero- and Trito-Isaiah (Isa. 40-55; 55-66), who during and immediately after the Exile are expecting Yahweh as redeemer (*go'el*): (Isa. 41:14; 43:14; 44:6, 24; 47:4; 48:17; 49:7, 26; 54:5, 8; 59:20; 60:16; 63:16).

Jonah gives thanks for his redemption. He has been saved from death by the great fish, but has he yet been saved from himself?

7 "When my *soul* fainted within me" is an unfortunate translation. Hebrew *nephesh* does not imply a division between body and soul, familiar to us from the Greek philosophical tradition. *Nephesh* is the complete person, Jonah's whole physical and spiritual being. In Jonah 2:7 Jonah has physically and spiritually come to the end of the road. The expression is stronger than Ps. 142:3: "When my *spirit* (*ruhi*) is faint."

At this point of complete despair Jonah remembers Yahweh. In Ps. 143:5 the psalmist remembers "the days of old" (also after "my spirit faints within me" in v. 4). This is a motif common to the Communal and Individual Laments. As for the people of Israel, Yahweh's previous acts of salvation are a source of new hope in adversity, so the individual worshipper recalls God's previous guidance and blessings and, on the strength of those, dares to ask him for help again. (For details cf. Westermann, *Praise and Lament in the Psalms,* 165-213.)

"And my prayer came to thee." God has to *hear* the request first, before he can *save*: "Let my prayer come before thee, incline thy ear to my cry!" prays the psalmist in Ps. 88:2.

"Into thy holy temple": Jonah, in the belly of the fish, directs his prayer to the temple of his God, which is in Jerusalem.

8 In this verse the psalm reaches an ironic climax. Is it really worshippers of "vain idols" who "forsake their true loyalty," i.e., Yahweh, who is loyal to them? What we have before us is a prophet who fears "the LORD, the God of heaven, who made the sea and the dry land" (Jonah 1:9), but a prophet who is running away from this very same God. By contrast, the narrator paints a picture of worshippers of "vain idols" who have come to fear Yahweh, to offer sacrifices, and to make vows (v. 16).

Like an "echo" (Magonet, 54) Ps. 31:6 comes through: "Thou hatest those"—rather than "I hate"—"who pay regard to vain idols; but I trust in the LORD!" A quotation after Jonah's own heart! The narrator continues in this verse to paint his picture of the self-righteous Jonah, who is still quite unaware of the real situation: Pagans have come to worship Yahweh, while Yahweh's prophet forsakes the one who is loyal to him!

9 "But I" (*wa'ani,* repeated from v. 4) again indicates Jonah's self-centeredness. He is different from those worshippers of "vain idols"!

He will *sacrifice* to Yahweh "with a voice of thanksgiving" (cf. Ps. 116:17)—it was the sailors who actually performed sacrifices (Jonah 1:16). What he has vowed he will pay (cf. Ps. 116:18)—it was the sailors, however, who made vows to Yahweh after their deliverance from the tempest.

"Deliverance belongs to the LORD!" (cf. Ps. 3:8)—this is exactly what the sailors understood, and *they* acted accordingly.

Through the use of irony (Magonet) our narrator describes Jonah as exactly the same self-centered character that he was in ch. 1 (against Wolff). He is still oblivious to the fact that the pagan sailors have adopted the behavior of true Yahweh worshippers, fulfilling all the criteria Jonah has set out in his psalm. He, on the other hand, condemns himself as one who has forsaken the one who is loyal to him; cf. David's self-condemnation ("You are the man") in 2 Sam. 12:7, and the implied self-condemnation of Isaiah's audience after the Song of the Vineyard (Isa. 5:1-7), when the prophet pulls the curtain aside in Isa. 5:7.

10 Yahweh now speaks to the fish, which is not a sea monster but a docile creature at his creator's command. After Jonah's punch line, "Deliverance belongs to the LORD," "the big fish throws up" (Holbert, 74). Jonah, the indigestible prophet, is quite unceremoniously vomited "upon the dry land" (*hayyabbashah),* whose Creator he had earlier confessed his God Yahweh to be (1:9).

Jonah now understands the implication of his confession "Creator of the sea and the dry land." This article of his faith has now been backed up by life experience. He cannot escape from his God, the Creator who is infinitely superior to all of his creatures, and even Tarshish is not out of his reach.

The word *(dabar)* of Yahweh has not been frustrated. Jonah has been saved, put back to the shores of Palestine, and the mission to Nineveh is still to go ahead. God's word prevails even where its messengers fail—a comforting thought for Church and Synagogue alike.

THE SECOND CALL
AND JONAH'S OBEDIENCE

3:1-3

Now Jonah receives his second call. The fact that Yahweh has not been impressed by Jonah's attempted flight and that Jonah's commission is still exactly the same as before can be seen from the almost complete identity of 3:1-2a with 1:1-2a.

1-2a This verse almost completely reproduces 1:1, apart from the fact that it omits Jonah's pedigree, ben Amittai, and introduces the Hebrew word *shenit*, "a second time." The call procedure is the same, and so is the message, which represents a direct repetition of 1:2a "Arise, go to Nineveh, that great city." Even the stereotyped formula "that great city" reappears, the author being as fond of it as Homer of his epithets, the decorative adjectives he attaches to all his leading personages.

2b Here the author introduces a minute variation: "proclaim to it" *(uqera' eleha)* for "cry against it" *(uqera' 'aleha)*. And now the author refers explicitly to the previous call, "the message that I tell you." To reemphasize the urgency and seriousness of the commission the author uses a *figura etymologica* that is unique in the OT: "proclaim the proclamation" *(qara' haqqeri'ah)*. Good narrative style prevents a repetition of the exact message that Jonah and the reader know only too well from ch. 1.

3a "So Jonah arose" again corresponds verbatim to 1:3, but this time not "to flee to Tarshish from the presence of the LORD." This time Jonah obeys completely; that is what is meant by *kidebar YHWH*.

The first scene of the second half of the book of Jonah (second call and obedience) is brief. This brevity, good narrative style—nothing superfluous is mentioned—does, however, invite the expositor to fill alleged gaps and introduce his own ideas.

To those who want to understand Jonah as a model prophet (e.g., Carl A. Keller), 3:3a provides an important argument: Jonah "goes in accordance with the word of the LORD." What more can we ask of him? But is his subsequent behavior in and outside Nineveh really "in accordance with the will of the LORD"? Is there not a distinction between the letter and spirit?—a distinction that Keller also ignores when comparing Jonah's death wish (4:8-9) with that of Elijah in 1 Kgs. 19:4 (Keller, "Jonas," 338). Is Jonah, still self-centered in the belly of the fish, now the model prophet? An unlikely story!

For those, from the church fathers to the exegetes of the Enlightenment, who want to see in Jonah the "typical, narrow-minded Jew," Jonah goes "reluctantly." Unfortunately for these expositors, the text does not say so. Jonah's silence must not be misconstrued.

The important point is that he *does* go, that he obeys. This simply implies that he has now existentially understood what he always "knew" from his religious tradition: Yahweh "made the sea and the dry land" (Jonah 1:9), and there is no fleeing from him to Tarshish. With Tarshish out of the way, Nineveh is Jonah's next stop.

3b So Jonah finds himself outside the gates of Nineveh. The longest period of *narrated* time, the journey, is reported in the briefest of *narrative* time (cf. Jacob Licht, *Storytelling in the Bible*, 96ff.). Nineveh "was a *great* city" (again the narrator's favorite word!), *le'lohim*—even by God's standards (cf. 4:11).

The description of the city as "three days journey in breadth (i.e., diameter)" shows that we have obviously left the realm of history. Ancient Nineveh, opposite modern Mosul on the left bank of the river Tigris, was 5 km. (3 mi.) long in its north-south extension, while, according to Hans Walter Wolff (*Obadiah and Jonah*, 148), "three days journey in diameter" would imply 60-80 km. (40-50 mi.). Historical Nineveh was destroyed by the Medes and Neobabylonians in 612 B.C.

The reference to Nineveh as a "great city" might put us on the right track since the Table of Nations adds after the mention of "Resen between Nineveh and Calah" the clarification "that is the great city" (Gen. 10:12). Disregarding the particular problems of Gen. 10:12, we may nevertheless safely conclude that our author thinks of Nineveh as one of the great cities of "once upon a time." His idea of a "king of Nineveh" (Jonah 3:6) on the analogy of, e.g., Abimelech king of Gerar (Gen. 20:2), implies little or no knowledge of historical Nineveh.

So now the scene is set for the real heart of the story—after the somewhat lengthy delay caused by our prophet. Jonah has now obeyed and seems set to take up his commission. What is he going to do? What is going to happen when he enters "enemy territory" and proclaims the *qeri'ah* with which he has been entrusted?

INSTANT SUCCESS IN NINEVEH

3:4-5

After devoting a whole chapter (ch. 2) to Jonah's sojourn of three days in the belly of the fish—the story was becoming incredibly slow (*narrative* time), considering the mere three days of *narrated* time!—our author moves on faster and faster. Jacob Licht (*Storytelling in the Bible*) gives further biblical examples for the slowing down (*ritardando*) in narrative of brief events and the rapid reporting (*accelerando,* my terms) of events of long duration (like Jonah's journey to Nineveh in 3:3).

4 Jonah now begins to go into the city, *one day's* journey. The author is not implying that Jonah goes *only* one day's journey into the city, still attempting to sabotage his commission. As can be seen from the result, one day's journey is perfectly sufficient for his message to spread rapidly around the city.

The stereotyped reference to "Nineveh, that great city," has been dropped. The *city* is no longer great, and *Nineveh* is to be overthrown!

Jonah now cries *(wayyiqera')* as he was bidden (1:2//3:2); he cries out God's announcement of judgment concerning Nineveh, and no longer about his own distress (2:2).

The announcement is brief: "Yet forty days, and Nineveh shall be overthrown!" There is no indictment. The *ra'ah,* "wickedness," of Nineveh (1:2) is not a matter of concern to our author. He is interested in Nineveh's *response* to Jonah's announcement of judgment. While he describes the announcement with utmost brevity, almost the whole of ch. 3 is given over to Nineveh's response.

In forty days' time Nineveh will be overthrown *(neheppaket).* This form is derived from the verb *haphak,* which occurs ninety-four times in the OT, and there are six occurrences of the noun *maheppekah.* The basic meaning of this root seems to be "to *turn, overturn*" (BDB). Its least ambiguous passage is probably Hos. 7:8, the turning of a cake.

However, in about 40 percent of all cases a change of some sort seems to be implied: mourning to joy (Jer. 31:13), feasts into mourning and songs into lamentations (Amos 8:10), justice into poison (Amos 6:12), darkness into morning (Amos 5:8), justice into wormwood (Amos 5:7), mourning into dancing (Ps. 30:11), the sea into dry land (Ps. 66:6), water into blood (Ps. 105:29), a curse into a blessing (Deut. 23:5; Neh. 13:2), the rod into a serpent (Exod. 7:15), the sun into darkness (Joel 2:31).

An equally large proportion has the meaning "to *turn,* to *turn around*": one's back to one's enemies (Josh. 7:8), the man from his chariot (2 Kgs. 5:26), food in one's stomach (Job 20:14), the earth (Job 28:5), mountains (Job 9:5), an inheritance over to strangers (Lam. 5:2), Pharaoh's mind towards the people (Exod. 14:5), God into an enemy (Isa. 63:10); and certainly the turning sword of Gen. 3:24. Sometimes this "turning" implies *overthrowing*: the mighty (Job 34:25), Jerusalem (2 Kgs. 21:13), a tent in the Midianite camp (Judg. 7:13).

Fifteen occurrences of the verb *haphak* or the noun *maheppekah* have the meaning "to destroy." The noun is used exclusively for the destruction of Sodom and Gomorrah (Deut. 29:23; Isa. 13:19; [cf. 1:7]; Jer. 49:18; 50:40; Amos 4:11). The verb refers seven times to the destruction of Sodom and Gomorrah (Gen. 19:21, 25, 29; Deut. 29:23; Jer. 20:16; Lam. 4:6; Amos 4:11). David's "comforters" are allegedly plotting the destruction of the capital of the Ammonites (2 Sam. 10:3), and Nineveh in the book of Jonah is to be destroyed like Sodom (cf. Joseph Blenkinsopp, "Abraham and the Righteous of Sodom," *JJS* 33 [1982]: 119-132).

While there can be no doubt that Jonah announces the destruction of Nineveh, there remains the possibility that his oracle could be ambiguous: "Yet forty days, and Nineveh will be *changed*"—be it through destruction or through penance. The many occurrences of *haphak,* "to change," suggest that there could be such an allusion in Jonah 3:4.

The continuation of the story, however, tells against this solution. Jonah for one regards his oracle as unambiguous. He has announced the destruction of Nineveh, and it has not taken place—whereas a change of heart on the Ninevites' part did occur! Yahweh also is not trying to persuade Jonah that the oracle has really been fulfilled because the Ninevites have done penance. God repented of the announced judgment, *"and he did not do it"* (v. 10).

5 Jonah's brief message meets with an instant response: the people of Nineveh *believe* in God. The Hebrew verb *he'emin* is the same as

in Gen. 15:6: "And (Abraham) believed the LORD; and he reck-
oned it to him as righteousness," and in Isaiah's oracle to Ahaz: "If
you will not believe, surely you shall not be established" (Isa. 7:9b).
In Gen. 15:6 it is Abraham, Israel's representative and ancestor, who
believes; in Jonah 3:5, the wicked pagans of Nineveh. While Ahaz
hesitates, the Ninevites respond immediately.

The Hebrew word used for the Ninevites, *"people* of Nineveh," is
the same as in Jonah 1, *ha'anashim.* In 1:10, 16 the *"men"* fear a
great fear, and in v. 13 they try to row back to the shore; they are no
longer called sailors as in v. 5, because of their ascent to God. The
same word is used to indicate the parallel ascent of the Ninevites.

The Ninevites believe in the *deity (elohim)* on whose behalf Jonah
has spoken. They do not know Yahweh, yet they believe. While it is
Yahweh who calls Jonah in 1:1//3:1, the divine name is avoided in
the mouth of the pagans. Chapter 3 is consistent with its use of
(ha)'elohim. The Ninevites believe in God (3:5); they are to call to
God (v. 8); perhaps the deity will turn and repent (v. 9); the deity
sees their deeds (v. 10); and the deity does repent (cf. Magonet,
Form and Meaning, 33-38).

The Ninevites *call a fast,* again the key verb *qara',* "to call." They
respond to Jonah's *qeri'ah,* "call/message" (3:2), by *calling a fast
(tsom).* Apart from v. 5, the technical term *qara' tsom* occurs six times
in the OT. A fast is called to trick Naboth, who is unwilling to sell
or swap his vineyard (1 Kgs. 21:9, 12). Jehoshaphat proclaims a fast
throughout all Judah before the battle against the Moabites and Ammonites (2 Chr. 20:3). The people of Jerusalem proclaim a fast in
the 5th year of Jehoiakim (Jer. 36:9), and so does Ezra at the river
Ahava (Ezra 8:21). Trito-Isaiah asks the postexilic Jewish congregation: "Will you call this a fast, and a day acceptable to the LORD?"
(Isa. 58:5).

As an external sign of their fast the Ninevites *put on sackcloth.* Joel
calls Israel to do penance: "Lament like a virgin girded with sackcloth . . ." (Joel 1:8); "Gird on sackcloth and lament, O priests, wail,
O ministers of the altar. Go in, pass the night in sackcloth, O ministers of my God!" (Joel 1:13).

The Ninevite fast is a popular movement including all social
classes "from the greatest of them to the least of them." Again the
narrator uses his favorite word *gadol,* "great." So far the parallel to
Jer. 36:9 holds good: the *people* of both Nineveh and Jerusalem proclaim a fast.

After a slow buildup—Jonah delaying his commission and
Yahweh taking successful countermeasures—the narrator reports

the conversion of Nineveh with as few words as possible: Jonah proclaims his message; the people proclaim a fast! No other prophet in the OT is as successful as Jonah. While Yahweh has allowed the city forty days for a change of mind, the Ninevites respond instantly. This shows the reader quite clearly that the problem is not the city of Nineveh. The problem is Jonah!

THE ROYAL RESPONSE

3:6-9

Jonah 3:5 describes the conversion of the Ninevites. Is it not Yahweh's turn now to respond? Our narrator, however, delays God's reaction by reporting after the people's response that of the king of Nineveh. As this seems unnecessary for the continuation of the story, what is the narrator's purpose in introducing the royal response?

The answer to this question can be found in Jer. 36, which, according to Hagia Witzenrath (*Das Buch Jona*, 89), is the negative foil for Jonah 3. The *people* of Jerusalem and Nineveh act in the same way by proclaiming a fast (3:5 // Jer. 36:9). But it is in the *royal* response (king of Nineveh/Jehoiakim) where the difference between the two chapters lies. While Jer. 36 records the rejection of the word of Yahweh (cf. Ernest W. Nicholson, *Preaching to the Exiles*, 39-45), Jonah 3 describes its surprising acceptance.

According to Witzenrath (*Das Buch Jona*, 89), Jer. 36 shows a Judaean king rejecting a prophet's call to do penance, while Jonah 3 shows a king—and a pagan one at that—doing penance together with all his people. While Baruch reads a complete scroll to people and king, Jonah only has to deliver a brief message—and it is effective! While Jerusalem is called to do penance, Nineveh receives only an announcement of its impending destruction.

The reading of the scroll produces no change of heart in Jerusalem, while, according to Witzenrath, a short message is enough to make the whole city of Nineveh turn. While Jehoiakim burns the scroll and attempts to arrest Jeremiah, the king's edict in Nineveh demands public acts of penance.

The unrepentant Jehoiakim is threatened with a new oracle of judgment. In Nineveh Yahweh repents of the evil and does not do it. Thus, the unrepentant Jehoiakim provides the contrast to the king of Nineveh and the pagans' fear of God.

6 The story of the *dabar* continues, reaching even the king of Nineveh. He, too, rises *(qûm),* not to run away from his responsibility like Jonah in Jonah 1:3, but to face up to it. Before ordering public acts of penance, he himself practices what he is going to preach.

He truly humbles himself, exchanging his throne for the dust. He removes his royal robe and puts on sackcloth. Similarly, Job rends his robe and falls to the ground (Job 1:20). What in Job is a mark of suffering is in the king of Nineveh's case a sign of penance. Common to Job 1 and Jonah 3 is the fact that both are performed as public gestures. Penance needs to be done and needs to be *seen* to be done!

7 The king *made proclamation.* The verb used is the hiphil form of *za'aq,* "to cry," also used of the sailors, each of whom cries to his god (1:5), another parallel between chs. 1 and 3. While the sailors cry in the face of the destruction of their ship, the king's men cry to avert the destruction of their city.

The proclamation formula is interesting: "By the decree of the king and his nobles (again the narrator's favorite word, *gadol*)," because it affects the dating of the book of Jonah. Neither in Israel nor in Assyria (at the time of Jonah ben Amittai) were proclamations issued "in the name of the king *and his nobles.*" But this was certainly the case during the Persian Empire. The Persian king had seven counselors or legal advisers. Ezra is told: "You are sent by the king and his seven counselors to make inquiries about Judah and Jerusalem according to the law of your God, which is in your hand" (Ezra 7:14). Esther 1:13-14 names "the seven princes of Persia and Media, who saw the king's face, and sat first in the kingdom" (cf. Herodotus *History* iii.31, 84, 118). Because of Jonah 3:7 this book cannot have been written before the 6th cent.

The decree applies to *humans* and *animals,* the latter being further specified as cattle and mixed flocks of *sheep* and *goats.* The animals are obviously important in the book of Jonah, because they reappear at the very end: "much cattle" (Jonah 4:11). Humans and animals belong much closer together for the ancient world than for modern thinking. In fairy tales humans and animals talk to each other (cf. Num. 22:28-30). This original unity of humans and animals goes right back to the act of creation. In Gen. 1 (P) the animals form part of the creation of the cosmos, which is crowned by the creation of mankind. In Gen. 2 (J) the animals are created as mankind's helpers.

Humans and animals are not to "taste anything," which is further specified: they are not to "feed" (on pastures) or even "drink water"

(Jonah 3:7). It is this original unity of humans and animals that involves even the animals in acts of penance.

8 Like the king of Nineveh, the citizens and even the animals are to cover themselves in *sackcloth* as a sign of mourning for their sins. According to Herodotus *History* ix.24, the Persian cavalry sheared themselves, their horses, and draught animals as a sign of mourning for the death of their leader.

Humans and animals are to cry—again the verb *qara'*—as loud as they can to (the unknown) God. In vain the captain had tried to persuade Jonah to cry to his God (Jonah 1:6), yet only in his "affliction" (2:2) had he got around to doing just that. Now after Jonah's *qeri'ah* to Nineveh (3:2) the Ninevites respond with a double *qara'*; they call a fast (v. 5), and they cry to God.

Each one is to *turn (shub)*. Hebrew *teshubah*, "penance," means that one turns from the wrong direction to the right one—like Greek *metanoein*, "to change one's mind," in the NT. The Ninevites *turn* in the hope that God may *turn*, i.e., "repent" (3:9). Hebrew *teshubah* is the subject of *Yom Kippur* in the Jewish religion, when the book of Jonah is read as the final lesson of afternoon prayers (Babylonian Talmud *Megillah* 31a).

Each person must turn from *his evil way*, i.e., "the violence which is in his hands." Hebrew *Derek hara'ah* (vv. 8, 10) means evil deeds of persons (cf. Digression II on *ra'ah* in 4:1).

9 "Who knows, (perhaps) the deity may turn and repent" (cf. Joel 2:14a). The proclamation still talks about an unknown deity. By rights Nineveh has no chance, but perhaps the impossible may yet happen. The unknown deity might be impressed by the acts of penance and the contrition of the Ninevites and turn and *repent (niham)*.

Jörg Jeremias has devoted a monograph to the subject of divine repentance *(Die Reue Gottes)*. He shows that, according to an older concept, God could repent even of acts of salvation for his people. Since Amos, however, divine repentance means that Yahweh saves his people from judgment that he himself had earlier determined to bring upon them. According to Jeremias, this "self-restraint" is understood, since the Exile, in such a way that human behavior triggers off Yahweh's action against himself. While Joel only calls Israel to turn back, so that they may be saved by Yahweh's "self-restraint," the book of Jonah expects its readers to share Yahweh's will to spare Israel with the Gentiles who are oppressing the Jews.

The edict hopes that God may yet "turn from his fierce anger, *so that we perish not (welo' no'bed)*"—taking up the captain's words from Jonah 1:6: "Perhaps the god will give a thought to us, that we do not perish." The parallelism of chs. 1 and 3 is even more marked in the cases of the captain and the king of Nineveh, respectively.

We now have a second reason for the account of the royal response following the popular one of 3:4-5. As the king of Nineveh serves as a contrast to Jehoiakim in Jer. 36, he is also intended as a parallel to the captain in Jonah 1. The combination of both motifs strengthens the argument of the book of Jonah: pagans outdo Israel in their repentance and fear of God (Gen. 20; Exod. 1:15-21).

THE DIVINE REPENTANCE

3:10

10a Now at last the time has come for Yahweh to react to the Ninevites' behavior. But strangely enough, the text says *"the deity saw their actions."* As a Jewish author is addressing Jewish readers, the avoidance of the divine name is difficult to explain. All I can suggest is that the narrator simply continues the usage of the edict for the rest of ch. 3. The king of Nineveh and his nobles simply refer to an unknown deity, like the captain in 1:6.

God sees that the Ninevites have "turned *from their evil way*"; i.e., v. 8b of the edict, "let everyone turn from his evil way," has been carried out. The Ninevites have *turned*; will God *turn*, too?

10b And the deity *does* repent *(wayyinnahem)*. According to our author, the Ninevites' acts of contrition have triggered off the divine repentance. The postexilic prophets announce judgment so that it does *not* have to be carried out. The complete *teshubah,* "turning," of the Ninevites has enabled God to relent.

As the Ninevites have turned from their "evil way," so God now turns from the evil that he had announced, the destruction of Nineveh (cf. Digression II on *ra'ah* 4:a). Jonah 3:10 contains the root *'asah,* "to do," three times: the *deeds* of the Ninevites, "the evil which he had said he would *do* to them," and the conclusion "he did not *do* it."

So the unlikely "perhaps" of the king of Nineveh has come true after all. God has taken note of the human acts of contrition, even those of pagans, and has revoked the judgment announced through his prophet.

But where does this leave Jonah, his prophet? "When a prophet speaks in the name of the LORD, if the word does not come to pass or come true, that is a word which the LORD has not spoken; *the prophet has spoken it presumptuously,* you need not be afraid of him" (Deut. 18:22; cf. Robert P. Carroll, *When Prophecy Failed*). So, according to Deut. 18:22, Jonah looks like a false prophet and a paper tiger: the word spoken by him has not come true! And Yahweh looks like he is improving his reputation at Jonah's expense. Jonah reluctantly agreed to join in this game—but now the rules have been changed!

JONAH'S OUTBURST

4:1-4

1 Not surprisingly Jonah "blows his top":

> 1a And there came unto Jonah a great *ra'ah (figura etymologica)*
> 1b and he was angry.

What we have before us is a synthetic parallelism (v. 1a//v. 1b), which means that Jonah's *ra'ah* in v. 1a must be something similar to his *anger* in v. 1b. The RSV translation, "But it displeased Jonah exceedingly," hardly does it justice. This translation is influenced by the other occurrence of the *figura etymologica, ra'a' ra'ah,* in Neh. 2:10, where the meaning is indeed "displeasure": "But when Sanballat the Horonite and Tobiah the servant, the Ammonite, heard this, it displeased them greatly that someone had come to seek the welfare of the children of Israel."

However, the constructions used in Jonah 4:1 and Neh. 2:10 are different: in Jonah 4:1 the *ra'ah comes unto (el)* someone; in Neh. 2:10 someone *has* (the preposition *le) ra'ah*. We cannot, therefore, automatically assume that the meaning of *ra'ah* in Jonah 4:1 and Neh. 2:10 must be the same, as the constructions are different and there are only these two examples. It would make more sense, before committing ourselves, to have a look at the other usages of *ra'ah* (and particularly *ra'ah gedolah*) in the OT.

DIGRESSION II

Ra'ah—Evil, Calamity, Divine Punishment, Wickedness

As will be shown in the following, *ra'ah* has four different meanings in the OT: (1) evil deeds of persons; (2) human calamity; (3) God's actual or intended punishment; and (4) a human mental attitude (displeasure or wickedness?). There are 319 occurrences of *ra'ah* in the OT. In the majority of cases *one* meaning is clearly dominant, but sometimes two shades of meaning can be found, e.g., human calamity (2), following from divine punishment (3), or human wickedness (4), expressing itself in evil deeds (1).

1. Jonah 1:2 mentions the *ra'ah* of the Ninevites that has come before Yahweh. While this implies their wickedness as a mental attitude, it is predominantly what they have *done* that provokes Yahweh's anger, i.e., their misdeeds (referred to as *hatta'tam,* "sins," in the similar case of the Sodomites [Gen. 19:20]). These misdeeds the book of Jonah refers to as *derek hara'ah* in Jonah 3:8, 10—a wicked way of life, so to speak.

A whole collection of such *ra'ot* is given by Jeremiah in Jer. 44:9, which lists the crimes of the kings of Judah and of their wives, of the house of Israel and of Samaria, as well as the crimes of his audience and of *their* wives.

One of the technical terms for dealing out evil is *gamal ra'ah.* Joseph's brothers have dealt out evil to him (Gen. 50:15, 17). The Jerusalemites have brought it upon themselves (Isa. 3:9), and the book of Proverbs warns not to contend with a man who has done one no harm (Prov. 3:30). While David has repaid Saul good, Saul has repaid him evil (1 Sam. 24:17).

A further phrase for misdeeds is the *doing* of evil (*'asah ra'ot*). Jeremiah castigates his people for two *ra'ot*: they have forsaken Yahweh and have made useless substitutes for themselves (Jer. 2:13); there is a more summary indictment in Jer. 3:5. Ezekiel also uses the phrase for Israel's misdeeds (Ezek. 6:9; 20:43).

Also common is the phrase *shillem ra'ah tahat tobah,* to recompense evil for good (cf. Joseph's question to his brothers [Gen. 44:4] and the rhetorical question of Jeremiah [Jer. 18:20]). The psalmists also complain about being recompensed evil for good (Ps. 35:12; 38:20). Cf. Jer. 51:24, where the Babylonians are threatened with retribution for their evil deeds against Zion.

Finally the OT refers to the *planning* of evil deeds (*hashab ra'ah*), e.g., Joseph in his comment that the brothers' planning of evil has been turned into good by God (Gen. 50:20). Jeremiah speaks of the planning of evil against Heshbon (Jer. 48:2). One who planned evil against Yahweh came out from Nineveh according to Nah. 1:11. And the psalmist's enemies are planning evil against him (Ps. 41:7); the RSV translation, "they imagine the worst for me," is unlikely, as the other occurrences of *hashab ra'ah* show.

2. This usage relates to evil in the form of human calamity, misfortune, woe, and suffering. In Jonah 1:7-8 the sailors ask twice on whose account this great evil has come upon them. Characteristic is

the phrase, though absent in Jonah, *ba'ah ra'ah,* indicating that evil or misfortune has "come upon" someone. In Isa. 47:11 Deutero-Isaiah pronounces judgment on Babylon; evil shall come and disaster shall fall upon it. Jeremiah regards Israel as the first fruits of Yahweh's harvest: all who ate of it became guilty; evil came upon them (Jer. 2:3).

Evil, calamity, and misfortune have often been decided in advance against somebody: *kaletah hara'ah,* evil has been *determined:* against David by Saul (1 Sam. 20:7, 9); against Nabal (1 Sam. 25:17); and against Haman by King Ahasuerus (Esth. 7:7).

Several passages refer to the *seeing* of evil and calamity *(ra'ah ra'ah)*: 2 Kgs. 22:20//2 Chr. 34:28; Ps. 90:15; Prov. 22:3//27:12, where a prudent man sees danger and hides himself; Eccl. 5:13; 6:1//10:5, the evil that Koheleth has seen under the sun; Jer. 44:17; Neh. 2:17.

On six occasions the OT refers to an evil *day* or day of calamity *(yom ra'ah):* Ps. 27:5, where the psalmist expects Yahweh's protection in the day of trouble; 41:1; Prov. 16:4; Eccl. 7:14; Jer. 17:17-18; 51:2. A corresponding phrase *('et ra'ah)* indicates the *time* of trouble/calamity: Ps. 37:19; Eccl. 9:12; Jer. 2:27-28; 11:12; 15:11; Amos 5:13, "for it is an evil time," recurs verbatim in Micah 2:3.

3. The third usage is related to Yahweh's punishment that he intends to bring or actually brings upon somebody. In Jonah 3:10 God repents of the punishment against the Ninevites because of their penance—just the kind of thing Jonah had always been expecting from this God of his (Jonah 4:2).

Such divine punishment is often indicated by the phrase *hebi' ra'ah,* to *bring* evil upon somebody, e.g., in 1 Kgs. 21:21, 29, where Ahab is to be punished for the murder of Naboth, whose vineyard he has illegally acquired.

There are nineteen examples of *ra'ah* as divine punishment in the book of Jeremiah alone (e.g., Jer. 1:14; 32:23; 36:3; 42:17; 44:2, 23; 51:60, 64; "this great evil": 16:10; 32:42). Most of these passages describe Yahweh's punishment of Israel's unfaithfulness and of Babylon's opposition to him, respectively. Five passages refer to the fact that Yahweh *relents* and withdraws his punishment *(niham 'al/el hara'ah),* as in the book of Jonah (Jer. 18:8; 26:3, 13, 19; 42:10). Four passages in Jeremiah refer to the evil that Yahweh has *spoken (dibber et-hara'ah):* Jer. 19:15; 35:17; 36:31; 40:2, in all four cases against Judah and Jerusalem.

4. Finally, the book of Jonah refers to the great *ra'ah* that takes hold of Jonah (Jonah 4:1, 6). Is it just displeasure or discomfort

(RSV)? In v. 1 Jonah's *ra'ah (figura etymologica)* expresses itself in anger. This would suggest that Jonah has adopted a mental attitude of confrontation, of total opposition to God. Is he not almost possessed by the *ra'ah,* a kind of evil spirit from which Yahweh needs to *rescue* him *(lehatstsil)*? This indicates a psychological as well as a theological dimension to Jonah's *ra'ah.* Jonah is in a state of *ra'ah* until Yahweh, with the help of a castor oil plant, releases him therapeutically from that state. At this point Jonah is overcome by a great joy, *simhah gedolah (figura etymologica),* in v. 6.

Before a final decision on the translation of *ra'ah* in Jonah 4 is made, one might take a look at similar passages in the books of Jeremiah and Ezekiel. In Jer. 2:19; 22:22, *ra'ah* refers to Jerusalem's wickedness. This suggests to me the translation "this is because of your wickedness" in Jer. 4:18 too (against RSV). Jer. 23:11; 33:5 also refer to Jerusalem's wickedness. The same usage can be found in Ezek. 16:23. In one instance (1 Sam. 16:23) such a mental state is referred to as the *spirit* of evil *(ruah hara'ah)* afflicting Saul.

In the light of these prophetic parallels it would appear that the translations "displeasure" or "discomfort" miss the point. Jonah is not just uncomfortable, but rather is in a totally wrong mental attitude towards his God. His *ra'ah gedolah* in Jonah 4:1 is contrasted with the sailors' *yire'ah gedolah et-YHWH,* their great fear of the Lord *(figura etymologica;* 1:16), and the belief of the Ninevites (3:5). Jonah's *ra'ah* is opposition to Yahweh, as was the case with Jerusalem in Jeremiah's and Ezekiel's view, hence the translation "wickedness" would appear to be fully justified. The deliberate use of the *figura etymologica* lends further support to this argument. But in contrast to Jerusalem, Jonah is not to be *punished for,* but *rescued from* his wickedness. The divine irony breaks through his mental barrier (4:6-11).

Following the principle that Scripture is its own interpreter, it would appear that the forty-eight verses of the book of Jonah reflect all four usages of *ra'ah* in the OT. This strengthens the case for the translation of *ra'ah* in 4:1, 6 as "wickedness" rather than as "displeasure" or "discomfort."

---

1 (continued) Jonah is clearly in a state of *ra'ah,* in total opposition to Yahweh. This evil attitude—"wickedness" for want of a better word—has attacked him from the outside. Jonah needs to be released from his wickedness and his anger, from his total confrontational course to Yahweh. This Yahweh does in 4:6. While his re-

sentment at being cast in the role of a false prophet is understandable, Jonah now loses control of himself and becomes possessed by the *ra'ah*—and even here the narrator's favorite word *gadol* appears! The *ra'ah* expresses itself in fury and *anger*. Jonah is no longer himself.

2 In his outburst he "prays" to Yahweh—hardly the right word for what he has to say! The narrator, having returned to Jonah, also resumes the use of the divine name. And now, at last, he proceeds to reveal the reason for Jonah's flight (1:3), which, as a good storyteller who wants to keep his audience on tenterhooks, he has so far kept back.

Jonah had obviously given this whole matter a lot of thought when he was still back home "in his own country," i.e., on his native soil *(adamah)* in Gath-hepher in Galilee, and he fled to Tarshish for theological reasons!

He *knew (yada')* something about his God that made him run— as he also *knew* that he was the cause for the sailors' peril (1:12). Obviously, Jonah cannot yet cope with this knowledge. He is informed about his religious tradition, but fails to apply this knowledge to the case of Nineveh until he is instructed by Yahweh himself in 4:6-10.

Jonah *accuses* God of four things: "Thou art

(1) a gracious God and merciful,
(2) slow to anger,
(3) and abounding in steadfast love,
(4) and repentest of evil."

What Jonah quotes are elements of the liturgy. At least the first three can frequently be found in the Psalter, the Jewish prayer book: "But thou, O Lord, art a God merciful and gracious, slow to anger and abounding in steadfast love and faithfulness" (Ps. 86:15; cf. also Ps. 103:8; 145:8). This liturgical usage may also be reflected in Exod. 34:6, Yahweh's self-proclamation before Moses, "a God merciful and gracious, slow to anger, and abounding in steadfast love and faithfulness." That it formed part of the liturgy of the second temple community can be seen from its occurrence in the penitential prayer in Neh. 9:17, 31.

The only other passage to contain all four elements, however, is Joel 2:13: "Return to the LORD, your God, for

(1) he is gracious and merciful,
(2) slow to anger,
(3) and abounding in steadfast love,
(4) and repents of evil."

As we have already found that Jonah 3:9 (the edict) quotes Joel 2:14a, we have no doubt that it is Jonah who is dependent on Joel 2:13-14. While the quotations are used in two different places in the book of Jonah, they are logically held together in Joel by the verb *shub*, "to return": return to Yahweh so that he may turn and repent! In this case, we have to date Jonah slightly later than Joel.

While Hans Walter Wolff's claim (*Obadiah and Jonah*, 167) that Jonah's quotation is "cynical" goes too far, the prophet nevertheless voices a problem that many Jews must have seen in a similar light, e.g., Malachi's audience: "It is vain to serve God. What is the good of our keeping his charge or of walking as in mourning before the LORD of hosts? Henceforth we deem the arrogant blessed; evildoers not only prosper but when they put God to the test they escape" (Mal. 3:14-15). Is there any difference between those serving God and those that do not (Mal. 3:18)? "Where is the God of justice?" (Mal. 2:17).

That this is not just a postexilic problem is also evident from the Psalms of Lament, undatable as they are. Claus Westermann (*Praise and Lament in the Psalms*, 173-194) has drawn our attention to the so-called Foe Lament: "All the day my enemies taunt me, those who deride me use my name for a curse" (Ps. 102:8); "In the path where I walk they have hidden a trap for me" (Ps. 142:3b); "False witnesses have risen against me" (Ps. 27:12); and particularly close to our problem, "How long shall my enemy be exalted over me?" (Ps. 13:2).

There obviously came a point when for the common Israelite worshipper the prosperity or nondestruction of those who did not worship Yahweh became a problem. Jonah speaks for many, but not for a particular *party*.

For "repentest of evil" *(niham 'al hara'ah)* see above on Jonah 3:9 and Digression II on 4.1.

3 This verse contains Jonah's *death wish*. The nondestruction of Nineveh has self-destructive consequences for Jonah. As Yahweh did not fulfil his announcement, the firm foundation of the prophet's life seems to have vanished. Rather than face life under these circumstances, he wishes to die.

One thing Jonah never considers is the conversion and the saving of *Nineveh*. In his "prayer" (vv. 2-3) he says "I" nine times, thus demonstrating how completely self-centered he still is.

Our narrator uses a subtle irony in this verse, by putting Elijah's death wish (1 Kgs. 19:4b) into Jonah's mouth. While Elijah under the broom tree assumes that he has failed completely, Jonah's problem seems to be his success!

3b Jonah's claim, that death is better than life, reminds us of the grumbling of the Israelites against Moses in the desert: "Is it because there are no graves in Egypt that you have taken us away to die in the wilderness?" (Exod. 14:11).

4 Yahweh kindly asks Jonah to reconsider: "Do you do well to be angry?" Jonah's anger *(harah)* would have reminded every Jew who knew his Bible of Cain's *harah* (Gen. 4:5b). Here too, Yahweh intervenes to stop Cain: "Why are you angry, and why has your countenance fallen? If you do well, will you not be accepted (or "be able to lift up your face")? And if you do not do well, sin is couching at the door; its desire is for you, but you must master it" (Gen. 4:6-7).

Yahweh intervenes in both cases for a similar reason: he attempted to save Cain from the demon sin that was about to take possession of him just as he sought to save Jonah from his *ra'ah* (Jonah 4:6), i.e., from a hostile attitude to Yahweh—from a wickedness that possessed him.

Jonah 4:1-4 concludes with an open question. Jonah remains silent when challenged about his *ra'ah*. The self-centeredness of vv. 2-3 is unbroken. If Jonah is completely possessed by his *ra'ah*, then it is Yahweh who needs to *release* him therapeutically.

AN IRONIC INSTRUCTION
IN DIVINE PITY
4:5-11

Before Jonah's release can be effected, we need to be told what happened to him after his proclamation, since ch. 3 concerns itself with the more important response of the Ninevites. Now we are back with Jonah.

5 This verse contains a *Nachholung*: Jonah (in the meantime) had left the city and had sat down east of it. There he made himself a hut and sat under it until he saw what was going to happen to the city. Some exegetes place this verse after 3:4, but since there is no evidence for this in the biblical textual tradition, we shall have to interpret 4:5 exactly in the context in which we find it (cf. Norbert Lohfink, "Jona ging zur Stadt hinaus (Jon iv,5)," *BZ* 5 [1961]: 185-203).

After his outburst Jonah has settled down. The narrator does not tell us what Jonah expects to happen—there is again plenty of scope for the expositor's imagination and prejudice! While inside Nineveh acts of *teshubah* penance are going on, Jonah receives a private lesson about the nature of his God. While the pagans find their own way, the prophet needs to be instructed. The Jewish author seems to be asking ironically: can even Jews understand the will of Yahweh?

6 Jonah's release begins with another divine "appointment": the *qiqayon*, a castor-oil plant, *Ricinus communis.* This playful appointment of creatures by their Creator (worm and east wind are still to follow) is reflected in the use of *YHWH elohim*, "the LORD God," unique in the book of Jonah but used throughout Gen. 2-3, which speaks of mankind's creation by God and its alienation from him. The author of Jonah uses creation terminology to indicate the superiority of the Creator over his creatures!

Hans Walter Wolff argues (*Obadiah and Jonah*, 170) that *YHWH elohim* represents a transition from *YHWH* (Jonah 4:4) to *ha'elohim* (v. 7). The biblical evidence does not support this view. Apart from Jonah 4:6, there are forty-one occurrences of *YHWH elohim* in the

OT, twenty in Gen. 2-3 alone. This narrative uses *YHWH elohim* throughout. The only exception is the woman's conversation with the serpent, where—for understandable reasons—the divine name is avoided and only "God" is used (Gen. 3:1, 3, 5). It is therefore impossible to regard *YHWH elohim* in Gen. 2:4b as a transition from Gen. 1, where *elohim* is used, to Gen. 4:1, *YHWH*. This is also doubtful for the entire narrative Gen. 2-3 because of the "relapse" into *elohim* in Gen. 3:1, 3, 5.

In Exod. 9:30; Josh. 2:11; 2 Sam. 7:25; 2 Kgs. 19:19; Jer. 10:10, *YHWH elohim* is preceded and followed by *YHWH*. Hence it does not indicate a transition, but is simply a variant of *YHWH*, or *YHWH* is the subject of the sentence, while *elohim* forms part of the predicate.

Apart from Jonah 4:6, a transition from *YHWH* to *elohim* occurs only in 1 Chr. 17:16, and one from *elohim* to the divine name in Ps. 84:11; 1 Chr. 17:17. As Psalms and Chronicles frequently alternate between the divine name and other terms and designations, their limited evidence carries no weight. It is therefore best to understand Jonah 4:6 against the background of Gen. 2-3 and its creation terminology.

The *Ricinus,* a fast-growing plant with large leaves that is regarded as a weed by many Orientals, is raised up over Jonah's head to provide shade—or a "cooling-off period" for an irate prophet! The *Ricinus* is not in competition with Jonah's hut, since the hut does not seem to provide sufficient shade and coolness. Even if the *Ricinus* and the hut were in competition, removing Jonah 4:5 to a position after 3:4 does not solve the problem—unless one speculates on the forgetfulness of the reader.

The main purpose of the *Ricinus* is "to rescue Jonah from his wickedness," his hostile attitude. As we have argued above (see Digression II on 4:1), Jonah's *ra'ah* is a psychic or emotional state in which he is trapped and from which he needs to be released. This Yahweh effects with the *Ricinus.*

As a result, Jonah enters his new emotional state of "a great joy." The narrator contrasts Jonah's two emotions by the use of the *figura etymologica:* in 4:1 he "evils a great evil" *(ra'a' ra'ah)*; in v. 6 he "joys a great joy" *(samah simhah)*. In both emotional states Jonah is still self-centered, while the sailors, who "fear a great fear to the LORD" *(figura etymologica),* have become God-centered (1:16). With these stylistic tools the narrator provides important cross references.

The author's favorite word, *gadol,* "great," occurs for the penultimate time in Jonah's "great joy"—to reappear just one more time in Yahweh's concern for the "great city" (4:11).

7 The deity's next "appointment" produces a *worm* at dawn the following morning. Jonah's joy appears to have been short-lived. The humble worm "attacks" the *Ricinus* and it withers away. How is Jonah going to react?

8 We are not told immediately. The narrator slows down the story and increases our tension by reporting God's last "appointment": "a sultry *east wind*"! This is probably the *sirocco,* which comes from the desert ("east" meaning east of Palestine). Our author is familiar with the climate of Palestine, but has probably never been to Mesopotamia (Edwin M. Good, *Irony in the Old Testament,* 52). In addition to this stiffling sirocco, the *sun* beats upon Jonah's head so that he faints.

"How can a man function with a God like this, who favors his enemies but who, as soon as he has given one little thought to his servant's comfort, promptly makes life miserable for him again?" (Good, 52). These were probably Jonah's thoughts, because he repeats his death wish (v. 8bβ//3b).

To understand Jonah's repeated death wish, the expositor needs a feeling for the delicate overtones in the narrative, which I miss in Carl A. Keller, "Jonas." In my opinion, Keller compares purely verbatim, ignoring the overall significance of the context as well as the finer nuances and overtones. I fail to understand how one can place the self-inflicted loneliness of the "successful" Jonah outside the gates of Nineveh on the same level as the loneliness of Elijah, who is desperate about his apparent failure (Keller, 335ff.)—or how one can equate Elijah's death wish (1 Kgs. 19:4) with that of Jonah, who wishes to die because he is furious over the withering away of his *Ricinus* (Jonah 4:8-9; Keller, 338). Ignoring irony for fear of anti-Judaism leads Keller to a distortion of the image of Jonah into that of the "suffering servant" (cf. John C. Holbert, "Deliverance Belongs to Yahweh!", 80, n. 37).

9 After Jonah's first death wish (v. 3), Yahweh had asked the prophet: "Do you do well to be angry?" (v. 4). Now, after Jonah's second death wish, God asks him again with "the full force of divine irony" (Good, 53): "Do you do well to be angry *for the Ricinus?*" (v. 9a). And Jonah, like a stubborn child, yells: "Yes, and I am even

prepared to die for it!" "Could any satirist have drawn his portrait more deftly?" (Good, 53). Jonah is well and truly cornered!

10 But while Jonah has maneuvered himself into an absurd position, Yahweh still cares for him and does not let him go. With kindness and a good dose of ironic patience, he proceeds to teach Jonah a lesson from the *Ricinus:* "You are *concerned* about the *Ricinus.*" Hebrew *hus* normally is rendered "to pity" (RSV "you pity the plant"). In rabbinical Hebrew, however, *hus* means "to be concerned for one's property." (I owe this information to Alexander Rofé of the Hebrew University in Jerusalem.) This meaning, in my opinion, would fit perfectly in the book of Jonah: "You are concerned about the *Ricinus* as if it were your property"—in reality, however, "you did not labor (for it), nor did you make it grow (*giddalto,* the same root as the author's favorite word, *gadol,* "great")."

The plant "came into being (literally) as the son of one night, and *perished* as the son of one night." The verb *abad* connects the *Ricinus* with the captain's and the king's words: "that we may not perish *(welo' no'bed)*" (1:6//3:9). Does Jonah wish the sailors and the Ninevites to perish but is prepared to die for the *Ricinus?*

11 "And I," the Creator, "should not I be concerned for Nineveh," my property? "That great city"—a final echo of Jonah's commission (1:2//3:2)! In Nineveh there are, according to our author, more than 120,000 ignorant human beings "and also much *cattle*"! We could not do without the animals in this verse, because the mention of humans and animals together shows clearly that we are dealing with creation language. It is because Yahweh is the Creator that he is concerned for his creatures and has the right to restrain himself in the announced judgment.

This does not make Jonah a false prophet. The Creator's concern for his creatures is the most important feature of the divine mercy, and it may even necessitate that Yahweh does *not* carry out the judgment that his prophet has announced. Jonah confesses the faith of his ancestors in the creator of "the sea and the dry land" (1:9). But he has failed to understand the application of this article of faith to Yahweh's creatures in Nineveh.

In this respect, the book of Jonah speaks the same language as Gen. 1-11, the Psalms, and the Wisdom Literature. While Israel is God's chosen people, all humans (and animals!) are his creatures. They do not participate in Israel's election, but in God's *blessing* for all his creatures.

THE MESSAGE
OF THE BOOK OF JONAH

The book of Jonah is a book written *by a Jew for Jews*. As such it represents an attempt by a pious Jew to teach his co-religionists that after human contrition and penance the divine repentance and pardon can be extended even to the Gentiles. As such the book has no specifically "Christian" message, but the problems on which it sheds light in the relationship between religious "insiders" and "outsiders" are common to Judaism and Christianity: "Is your eye evil because I am good (to others)?" Jesus criticizes the religious "insider" (Matt. 20:15 RSV mg.).

The book of Jonah is not a tract or pamphlet directed against anybody. Scholarship has provided no convincing proof of a *party* that the author could be attacking. Rather than asking ourselves, who is the author getting at—not ourselves, of course!—we might do better by asking: what is the author trying to teach his contemporaries, and what can we learn from him?

For his new teaching the author has chosen the form of a *narrative,* which is unique among the "prophetic" books of the Bible but in keeping, e.g., with Nathan's parable (2 Sam. 12:1-15). The form of a story has been used for didactic and psychological reasons. Our author wants to stimulate a new way of thinking. He wants to provide an *internal self-correction* within Judaism.

Such a story is *multidimensional.* It can be understood on completely different levels. What is "just a good story" for one person can represent profound theological thinking for another. These levels are not mutually exclusive. One is not "right" and the other "wrong."

A narrative can also deal with more than one subject. From its center it sheds light on other aspects. The classical alternative of the two subjects, *either* "Jews and Gentiles" *or* "History of Prophecy," does not do justice to the *Gattung,* the classification, of the book of Jonah.

The book points, of course, to its main concern with God's final question to Jonah: "You are concerned for the *Ricinus,* for which you did not labor, . . . which came into being in a night, and perished in a night. And should I not be concerned about Nineveh, that great city, in which there are more than 120,000 persons who do not know their right hand from their left, and also much cattle?" The question to the reader is this: does God have a divine privilege of "repentance" when in the face of the announced judgment humans do penance—and this now for the first time applied to Gentiles?

As so often, Benno Jacob (*Das erste Buch der Tora*, 180) has already grasped the point: "It is the purpose of this book to show the fruit of penance and to teach man, who is even worried about a perishable plant, in his own fate and person *the divine privilege of mercy for all living beings.*" The philosopher Klaus Heinrich means basically the same thing when he refers to God's faithfulness to humanity (*Parmenides und Jona*).

We have already drawn the reader's attention to Jörg Jeremias' work on divine repentance, *Die Reue Gottes,* in connection with Jonah 3:9. According to Jeremias, this "self-restraint" is understood since the Exile in such a way that human behavior triggers off Yahweh's action against himself. Joel only calls *Israel* to turn back, so that they may be saved by Yahweh's "self-restraint." The book of Jonah, however, expects its readers to understand that Yahweh now wills to spare not only Israel but even the *Gentiles*—the very Gentiles who in postexilic times are oppressing the Jews. Our Jewish author shares the spirit of the Sermon on the Mount.

Now it becomes gradually apparent how the other themes of the book of Jonah are connected with the divine privilege of repentance: the exilic/postexilic understanding of divine repentance is based on a new concept of judgment prophecy. The latter is no longer understood as an irrevocable announcement of the future, but, according to Jeremias, as a warning in order to make Israel turn back so that Yahweh does not have to implement the acts of judgment with which he had threatened them.

Hence Jonah does *not* become a false prophet, according to Deut. 18:22, although his announcement has not been fulfilled. God's compassion for his creatures makes it necessary that he intervenes even against himself! God has changed his mind, and the prophet has—somewhat reluctantly, but in the end loyally—carried out his commission.

By extending the principle of divine repentance even to the Gentiles, the book of Jonah finally includes the subject "Jews/Gentiles." The sailors' fear of Yahweh (Jonah 1:16) directs our attention to other God-fearing Gentiles: in Gen. 20 Abimelech, king of Gerar, even exceeds Abraham in the fear of God. It is worth pointing out that the date of Gen. 20 is still uncertain; perhaps Jonah 1 and Gen. 20 are chronologically not that far apart! Exod. 1:15-21 describes the Egyptian midwives (cf. Brevard S. Childs, *The Book of Exodus*) as God-fearing, because they disobey Pharaoh and do not kill the Hebrew boys. Job, the Edomite (?), is also a biblical example of an unshakeable fear of God. It is therefore not unique in the OT when in Jonah 1 God-fearing pagans are held up as an example to Israel.

Why, however, is the divine repentance extended even to the Gentiles? It is because Jews and Gentiles (and much cattle!) are all God's creatures. Creation theology—linking Jonah to Gen. 1-11, the Psalms, and the Wisdom Literature—is what holds the book of Jonah together, without being its main theme. Because Jews and Gentiles are God's creatures, the divine repentance pertains to both of them. Because the Ninevites are God's creatures, he restrains himself in his action against them. And it is ultimately because of the superiority of the Creator over his creatures (cf. Job 38–41) that Yahweh can rescind the judgment announced, even after taking so much trouble in getting Jonah to announce it in the first place! (See the diagram, p. 128.)

The book of Jonah is an astonishing theological development. This is the type of postexilic Jewish theology in whose tradition Jesus of Nazareth stands. When Jesus describes humanity as ultimately dependent on divine forgiveness (e.g., Luke 15:11-32), he continues the tradition of the book of Jonah. This does not make the author of the book of Jonah a "secret Christian," but it identifies Jesus as a Jew who stands in the best tradition.

Judaism has identified itself with the theology of the book of Jonah by reading it at the important festival of Yom Kippur. That all humans are dependent on divine forgiveness is a basic axiom of Jewish and Christian *anthropology*. It is the *soteriological* question that we shall have to pursue in dialogue with our Jewish friends and partners: How far is that divine forgiveness bound up with the person of Jesus of Nazareth?

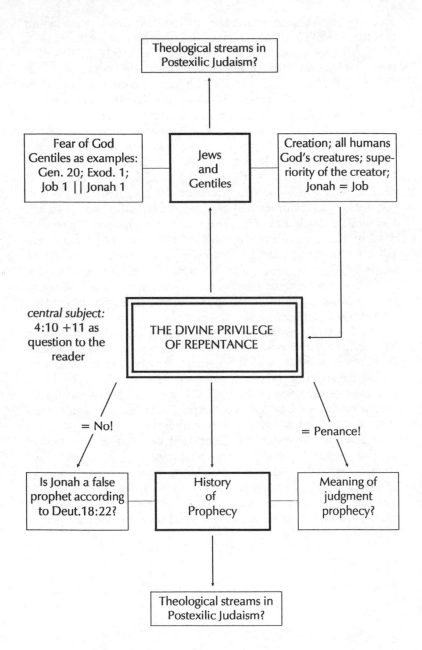

Theological streams in
Postexilic Judaism?

Fear of God
Gentiles as examples:
Gen. 20; Exod. 1;
Job 1 || Jonah 1

Jews
and
Gentiles

Creation; all humans
God's creatures; supe-
riority of the creator;
Jonah = Job

central subject:
4:10 +11 as
question to the
reader

THE DIVINE PRIVILEGE
OF REPENTANCE

= No!

= Penance!

Is Jonah a false
prophet according
to Deut.18:22?

History
of
Prophecy

Meaning of
judgment
prophecy?

Theological streams in
Postexilic Judaism?

128

EPILOGUE:
THE SIGN OF JONAH

The NT mentions the "sign of Jonah," but the Synoptic tradition gives us no clear indication of what exactly that means. NT scholars are also unsure whether Jesus himself spoke of the sign of Jonah or whether this expression was coined by the traditionists of the early Church (cf. A. Vögtle, "Der Spruch vom Jonaszeichen," *Synoptische Studien*, 230-277).

Matt. 12:38-41 equates Jonah's sojourn of three days and three nights in the belly of the fish with that of Jesus in the heart of the earth.

> (38) Then some of the scribes and Pharisees said to him, "Teacher, we wish to see a sign from you." (39) But he answered them, "An evil and adulterous generation seeks for a sign; but no sign shall be given to it except the sign of the prophet Jonah. (40) For as Jonah was three days and three nights in the belly of the whale, so will the Son of man be three days and three nights in the heart of the earth. (41) The men of Nineveh will arise at the judgment with this generation and condemn it; for they repented at the preaching of Jonah, and behold, something greater than Jonah is here."

However, it must be noted that the equation of the sign of Jonah with the three days and three nights in the belly of the fish is restricted to Matt. 12:40. The following verse seems to regard the preaching of Jonah as the sign to which the Ninevites responded. It is, therefore, possible that Matt. 12:40 is an expansion of the original saying: "We may then attribute to Matthew the elaboration of v. 40, making the experience of Jonah a symbol of the death and resurrection of Jesus; it is not related to the words about the appearance of the men of Nineveh at the Judgement, any more than to the appearance of the Queen of the South" (Francis W. Beare, *The Gospel According to Matthew*, 281-82).

This suggestion may find some support in *Matt. 16:4,* where the saying is quoted without an interpretation.

An evil and adulterous generation seeks for a sign, but no sign shall be given to it except the sign of Jonah.

Luke 11:29-32 regards the prophet's person as the sign.

> (29) When the crowds were increasing, he began to say, "This generation is an evil generation; it seeks a sign, but no sign shall be given to it except the sign of Jonah. (30) For as Jonah became a sign to the men of Nineveh, so will the Son of man be to this generation . . . . (32) The men of Nineveh will arise at the judgment with this generation and condemn it; for they repented at the preaching of Jonah, and behold, something greater than Jonah is here."

The *Markan version, Mark 8:11-13,* makes no reference to the sign of Jonah. While Mark 8:12 rejects *any* demand for a sign, the Q version in Matthew and Luke announces a sign, the sign of Jonah (cf. Walter Grundmann, *Das Evangelium nach Lukas,* 241-42). We may thus sketch the history of this saying as follows.

1. Mark 8:11-13 rejects the demand for *any* sign.
2. Q introduces the sign of Jonah (Matt. 16:4), the point of comparison being the *preaching* of Jonah and that of Jesus. While the former is successful, the latter is rejected.
3. While for Luke 11:29-32 the *person* of Jonah is the sign, corresponding to the person of Jesus (cf. Grundmann), in Matt. 12:38-41 the evangelist equates the sign of Jonah with the three days and three nights in the belly of the fish—the point of comparison being Jesus's sojourn in the grave.

It would, therefore, appear that Jesus radically rejects the demand for *any* sign, while the early Church compares his *preaching* to the sign of Jonah. The interpretation of the sign as the *person* of Jonah and of Jesus on the one hand, and as the "three days and three nights" on the other are the work of Luke and Matthew, respectively (cf. Richard A. Edwards, *The Sign of Jonah in the Theology of the Evangelists and in Q).*

This said, we ought to consider the relationship of OT exegesis to that of the NT. Quotations of the OT in the NT or more general references such as the sign of Jonah do not help us to understand the original intention of the OT authors. Rather, they have become part of what the NT authors have to say. Often the NT interpretation is in conflict with the original meaning of the OT text.

It therefore makes more sense to read the NT against the background of the OT. When the meaning of an OT text, such as the book of Jonah, has been determined, we may *then* ask whether the NT stands in continuity or discontinuity with its message.

Thus it becomes apparent that the Jonah theme continues in the parables of Jesus, where it plays a much more important part than in the ambiguous reference to the sign of Jonah. Divine forgiveness for the religious "outsider," with the "insider" looking on grudgingly, is a frequent subject in Jesus' parables.

The parable of the unmerciful servant (Matt. 18:23-35) portrays a "Jonah" figure. Like Jonah, who has been pardoned for his disobedience and has been saved from death by Yahweh, but is still unwilling to see Nineveh receive forgiveness, so the unmerciful servant is unwilling to forgive his fellow servant a petty debt, although he has received much greater forgiveness from his master. "The general theme, of course, goes back to Jesus: he expects God's free forgiveness to be reflected in our readiness to forgive others" (Beare, 383).

In the parable of the prodigal son (Luke 15:11-32), the elder brother is the Jonah figure. He who has been a dutiful son all the time now begrudges the prodigal his undeserved forgiveness. Gerhard von Rad, perhaps inspired by his knowledge of the book of Jonah, once preached on Luke 15:11-32 as the "parable of the *two lost sons*" (Gerhard von Rad, *Predigten,* 120-26). It is the elder brother in this parable who is the really problematic character.

The parable of the Pharisee and the tax collector (Luke 18:9-14) represents the Pharisee as a Jonah figure and the tax collector as a "Ninevite," an outsider. The Pharisee prays: "God, I thank thee that I am not like other men, extortioners, unjust, adulterers, or even like this tax collector. I fast twice a week, I give tithes of all that I get" (Luke 18:11-12). The tax collector, like the king of Nineveh who also hopes against all odds, prays: "God, be merciful to me a sinner!" (Luke 18:13). As in the book of Jonah, the narrator approves of the humble outsider.

In the parable of the laborers in the vineyard (Matt. 20:1-16) the "Jonahs" have "borne the burden of the day" (Matt. 20:12), while the "Ninevites" have been idle until the "eleventh hour." Here, too, the insiders begrudge the outsiders the householder's kindness. As Jonah is rebuffed with the example of the *Ricinus,* the householder questions the men of the first hour: "Do you begrudge my generosity?" (Matt. 20:15). "There is probably behind this the general doctrine that the rewards of God are not measured out according to length of time that we have served him; perhaps also that the Gentiles, who are only now entering the service of God, will not fare less well than Israel, which has come through centuries of hardship" (Beare, 404).

The story of Jonah is the story of the religious "insider"—in post-exilic Israel, at the time of Jesus, and today in the Synagogue as well as in the Church.

BIBLIOGRAPHY

Books

Ben-Chorin, Schalom. *Die Antwort des Jona zum Gestaltwandel Israels* (Hamburg: Herbert Reich, 1956).

Bickerman, Elias J. *Four Strange Books of the Bible* (New York: Schocken, 1967).

Cohn, Gabriel H. *Das Buch Jona im Lichte der biblischen Erzählkunst.* Studia Semitica Neerlandica (Assen: Van Gorcum, 1969).

Edwards, Richard A. *The Sign of Jonah in the Theology of the Evangelists and in Q.* Studies in Biblical Theology, 2nd ser. (London: SCM and Naperville: Allenson, 1971).

Haller, Eduard. *Die Erzählung von dem Propheten Jona.* Theologische Existenz heute 65 (Munich: Chr. Kaiser, 1958).

Heinrich, Klaus. *Parmenides und Jona* (Frankfurt: Suhrkamp, 1966).

Magonet, Jonathan D. *Form and Meaning: Studies in Literary Techniques in the Book of Jonah* (1976; repr. Sheffield: Almond, 1983).

Steffen, Uwe. *Jona und der Fisch: Der Mythos von Tod und Wiedergeburt* (Stuttgart: Kreuz, 1982).

Werner, Herbert. *Jona: Der Mann aus dem Ghetto.* Exempla Biblica 2 (Göttingen: Vandenhoeck & Ruprecht, 1966).

Witzenrath, Hagia. *Das Buch Jona: Eine literaturwissenschaftliche Untersuchung.* Arbeiten zu Text und Sprache im Alten Testament 6 (St. Ottilien: Faculty of Catholic Theology, University of Munich, 1978).

Wolff, Hans Walter. *Obadiah and Jonah: A Commentary* (Minneapolis: Augsburg and London: SPCK, 1986).

———. *Studien zum Jonabuch,* 2nd ed. Biblische Studien 47 (Neukirchen-Vluyn: Neukirchener Verlag, 1975).

Articles

Brenner, Athalja. "The Language of Jonah as an Index of Its Date," *Beth Mikra* 24 (1979): 396-405 [in Hebrew].

Budde, Karl. "Vermutungen zum 'Midrasch des Buches der Könige,'" *Zeitschrift für die Alttestamentliche Wissenschaft* 12 (1892): 37-51.

Burrows, Millar. "The Literary Category of the Book of Jonah," in *Translating and Understanding the Old Testament,* ed. Harry Thomas Frank and William L. Reed (Nashville: Abingdon, 1970), 80-107.

Clements, Ronald E. "The Purpose of the Book of Jonah," *Supplements to Vetus Testamentum* 28 (1975): 16-28.

Emmerson, Grace I. "Another Look at the Book of Jonah," *Expository Times* 88 (1976/1977): 86-88.

Galling, Kurt. "Der Weg der Phöniker nach Tarsis in literarischer und archäologischer Sicht," *Zeitschrift des Deutschen Palästina-Vereins* 88 (1972): 1-18, 140-181.

Golka, Friedemann W. "Jonaexegese und Antijudaismus," *Kirche und Israel* (1986), 51-61.

Holbert, John C. "'Deliverance Belongs to Yahweh!': Satire in the Book of Jonah," *Journal for the Study of the Old Testament* 21 (1981): 59-81.

Kaiser, Otto. "Wirklichkeit, Möglichkeit und Vorurteil: Ein Beitrag zum Verständnis des Buches Jona," *Evangelische Theologie* 33 (1973): 91-103.

Keller, Carl A. "Jonas: Le portrait d'un prophète," *Theologische Zeitschrift* 21 (1965): 329-340.

Landes, George M. "Linguistic Criteria and the Date of the Book of Jonah," *Eretz Israel* 16 (1982): 147*-170*.

Lohfink, Norbert. "Jona ging zur Stadt hinaus (Jon iv,5)," *Biblische Zeitschrift* 5 (1961): 185-203.

Payne, David F. "Jonah from the Perspective of its Audience," *Journal for the Study of the Old Testament* 13 (1979): 3-12.

Pesch, Rudolf. "Zur konzentrischen Struktur von Jona 1," *Biblica* 47 (1966): 577-581.

von Rad, Gerhard. "Der Prophet Jona," in his *Gottes Wirken in Israel,* ed. Odil H. Steck (Neukirchen-Vluyn: Neukirchener Verlag, 1974), 65-78.

Schmidt, Ludwig. *'De Deo,' Beihefte zur Zeitschrift für die Alttestamentliche Wissenschaft* 143 (1976).

Soggin, Juan Alberto. "Il 'segno del Giona' nel libro del profeta Giona," *Lateranum* 48 (1982): 70-74.

Vögtle, A. "Der Spruch vom Jonaszeichen," in *Synoptische Studien* (Munich: K. Zink, 1953), 230-277.

Weimar, Peter. "Jonapsalm und Jonaerzählung," *Biblische Zeitschrift* 28 (1984): 43-68.

West, Mona. "Irony in the Book of Jonah: Audience Identification with the Hero," *Perspectives in Religious Studies* 11 (1984): 233-243.

Other Works

Beare, Francis W. *The Gospel According to Matthew* (1981; repr. Peabody, MA: Hendrickson, 1987).

Blenkinsopp, Joseph. "Abraham and the Righteous of Sodom," *Journal of Jewish Studies* 33 (1982): 119-132.

―――. "Old Testament Theology and the Jewish-Christian Connection," *Journal for the Study of the Old Testament* 28 (1984): 3-15.

Carroll, Robert P. *When Prophecy Failed* (London: SCM and New York: Seabury, 1979).

Childs, Brevard S. *The Book of Exodus.* Old Testament Library (Philadelphia: Westminster and London: SCM, 1974).

Feinberg, Leonard. *Introduction to Satire* (Ames: Iowa State University Press, 1967).

Fokkelman, Jan P. *Narrative Art and Poetry in the Books of Samuel,* 1: *King David.* Studia Semitica Neerlandica 20 (Assen: Van Gorcum, 1981).

Good, Edwin Marshall. *Irony in the Old Testament* (Philadelphia: Westminster and London: SPCK, 1965).

Greenberg, Moshe. "Mankind, Israel and the Nations in the Hebraic Heritage," in *No Man is an Alien,* ed. J. Robert Nelson (Leiden: Brill, 1971), 15-40.

Grundmann, Walter. *Das Evangelium nach Lukas,* 2nd ed. Theologisches Handkommentar zum Neuen Testament (Berlin: Evangelische Verlagsanstalt, 1961).

Hanson, Paul D. *The Dawn of Apocalyptic,* 2nd ed. (Philadelphia: Fortress, 1975).

Heidel, Alexander. *The Babylonian Genesis: The Story of Creation* (Chicago and London: University of Chicago Press, 1963).

Jacob, Benno. *Das erste Buch der Tora, Genesis* (1934; repr. New York: Ktav, 1974).

Jeremias, Jörg. *Die Reue Gottes: Aspekte alttestamentlicher Gottesvorstellung* (Neukirchen-Vluyn: Neukirchener Verlag, 1975).

Kraus, Hans-Joachim. *Psalmen 1-59,* 5th ed. Biblischer Kommentar Altes Testament (Neukirchen-Vluyn: Neukirchener Verlag, 1978).

Licht, Jacob. *Storytelling in the Bible* (Jerusalem: Magnes, 1978).

Nicholson, Ernest W. *Preaching to the Exiles: A Study of the Prose Tradition in the Book of Jeremiah* (Oxford: Blackwell, 1970).

Orlinsky, Harry M. "Nationalism-Universalism and Internationalism in Ancient Israel," in *Translating and Understanding the Old Testament* (Nashville: Abingdon, 1970), 206-236.

Plöger, Otto. *Theocracy and Eschatology* (Oxford: Blackwell, 1968).

von Rad, Gerhard. *Predigten,* ed. Ursula von Rad (Munich: Christian Kaiser Verlag, 1972).

Rendtorff, Rolf. *Das überlieferungsgeschichtliche Problem des Pentateuch,* Beihefte zur Zeitschrift für die Alttestamentliche Wissenschaft 147 (1977).

Rofé, Alexander. "Classes in the Prophetical Stories: Didactic Legenda and Parable," *Supplements to Vetus Testamentum* 26 (1974): 143-164.

Smend, Rudolf. *Die Entstehung des Alten Testaments* (Stuttgart: Kohlhammer, 1978).

Smith, Morton. *Palestinian Parties and Politics that Shaped the Old Testament* (New York and London: Columbia University Press, 1971).

Steck, Odil Hannes. "Das Problem theologischer Strömungen in nachexilischer Zeit," *Evangelische Theologie* 28 (1968): 445-458.

Westermann, Claus. *Genesis 1-11: A Commentary* (Minneapolis: Augsburg and London: SPCK, 1984).

————. *Praise and Lament in the Psalms* (Atlanta: John Knox and Edinburgh: T. & T. Clark, 1981).